Bottles of Delight

Bottles
of
Delight

THE THAI COLLECTION
of Chinese Snuff Bottles

Jennifer Chen

with an introduction by Robert Hall

Seattle Art Museum

Published by the Seattle Art Museum

Distributed by Art Media Resources, Ltd., Chicago

Internet *http://www.webart.com/artmedia*

Edited by Suzanne Kotz
Designed by John Hubbard
Produced by Marquand Books, Inc., Seattle
Photography by Paul Macapia

Front cover: left, detail, porcelain snuff bottle, 19th c. (cat. no. 1);
right, inside-painted snuff bottle, 1895, by Ding Erzhong (cat. no. 38)
Back cover: single overlay glass snuff bottle, 1750–1800 (cat. no. 27)
Frontispiece, left to right: detail, porcelain snuff bottle, 19th c. (cat. no. 1);
agate snuff bottle, 1750–1860 (cat. no. 19); porcelain snuff bottle, 19th c.
(cat. no. 2); inside-painted snuff bottle, 1923 (cat. no. 44); single overlay
glass snuff bottle, 19th c. (cat. no. 29); inkstone snuff bottle, early 19th c.
(cat. no. 24)

Library of Congress Cataloging-in-Publication Data
Chen, Jennifer.
    Bottles of delight : the Thal collection of Chinese snuff bottles /
Jennifer Chen ; with an introduction by Robert Hall.
       p.   cm.
    ISBN 0-932216-49-8 (pbk. : alk. paper)
    1. Snuff boxes and bottles—China—Catalogs. 2. Decorative arts—
China—Ming–Ch'ing dynasties, 1368–1912—Catalogs. 3. Thal, Sidney—
Art collections—Catalogs. 4. Snuff boxes and bottles—Private collections
—Washington (State)—Seattle—Catalogs. 5. Snuff boxes and bottles—
Washington (State)—Seattle—Catalogs. 6. Seattle Art Museum—Catalogs.
I. Seattle Art Museum. II. Title.
NK9507.C52   1998
745.593'4'074797772—dc21   98-10907

PRINTED IN HONG KONG

Contents

Foreword

CHINESE SNUFF BOTTLES ARE INTRIGUING WORKS OF ART, whether featuring a superbly carved branch of blossoming plum, a poetic landscape painting, or the natural beauty of a translucent stone. They are a microcosm of the artistic achievements of the Qing dynasty (1644–1911).

In 1996, to honor Sidney and Berta Thal, Stephen and Britt Thal gave their fine collection of fifty Chinese snuff bottles and one jadeite carving to the Seattle Art Museum. The Thal collection, especially its inside-painted snuff bottles, complements our existing holdings, creating an area of strength in the Chinese collection to be enjoyed by generations of visitors to the Seattle Asian Art Museum, where they are on continuous display.

Sidney Thal, with his late wife, Berta, has long been a beloved and admired member of the Seattle community. Among other endeavors, in 1948 they purchased Fox's Gem Shop in the heart of downtown Seattle. As a child, their son Stephen frequented the Seattle Art Museum in Volunteer Park and came to collect snuff bottles. The gift of Stephen and Britt Thal in honor of Sidney and Berta is intended for the enjoyment and appreciation of the citizens of Seattle.

For this publication, particular recognition is due to Robert Hall, one of the leading authorities in the field, and Jennifer Chen, a talented young scholar of Chinese art. Mr. Hall wrote the introduction while Ms. Chen was responsible for the individual catalogue entries and oversaw photography.

Sidney and Berta Thal, parents of Stephen Thal

Stephen and Britt Thal

We also owe a debt of appreciation to everyone on the Seattle Art Museum staff who assisted with the project. William Rathbun, John A. McCone Foundation Curator of Asian Art, played an important role from the outset. Trevor Fairbrother, Deputy Director for Art and the Jon and Mary Shirley Curator of Modern Art; Gail Joice, Senior Deputy Director for Museum Services; and Jay Xu, Foster Foundation Associate Curator of Chinese Art, provided unfailing support in every step of research and publication. Paul Macapia was responsible for the outstanding photography, librarians Elizabeth de Fato and Jan Hwang were instrumental in locating research materials, and Zora Hutlova Foy did a superb job of coordinating the publication.

The handsome design of the catalogue is the work of John Hubbard and Ed Marquand, while Suzanne Kotz skillfully edited the text. They deserve credit for the excellence of their work and their good humor.

The museum extends special gratitude to Sidney Thal for generously supporting the publication of this catalogue of the Thal collection of Chinese snuff bottles. The collection embodies a great variety of technical and artistic achievements, and in the present volume, the bottles are classified into six groups: porcelain, jade, quartz, stone and amber, glass, and inside-painted. The beauty of each individual bottle is described in detail, and the symbolic meaning of its decoration is discussed. By increasing our understanding of artistic approaches in snuff bottle design and the relationship with other art forms, the authors have made a meaningful new addition to snuff bottle literature while celebrating the splendid gift of the Thal collection to the Seattle Art Museum.

Mimi Gardner Gates
The Illsley Ball Nordstrom Director

Chinese Snuff Bottles

IN THE RICH TAPESTRY OF CHINA'S ART HISTORY, snuff bottles occupy a unique place, the importance of which has only recently begun to be recognized. Although these small flasks are the products of only a single dynasty, the Qing (1644–1911), their makers were able to draw upon all the wealth of an uninterrupted tradition of artistic development going back thousands of years. Because of the extraordinary variety of styles, techniques, and materials to be found in these small objects, and the incredible craftsmanship that was lavished upon them, these miniature masterpieces became one of the most important representations of the applied arts during the Qing dynasty.

The tobacco plant is indigenous to both North and South America, whose native inhabitants smoked, chewed, and snuffed it for several centuries before Europeans discovered the New World. Brought to Europe by early travelers to the Americas at the end of the fifteenth century, the tobacco plant was quickly spread around the rest of the known world by merchants and mariners. During the last half of the sixteenth century, it was introduced into the Philippines, then known as Luzon, by the Spaniards, and into Japan by the Portuguese.

When it arrived in China toward the end of the sixteenth century, tobacco was at first smoked in long pipes with tiny bowls. The habit was taken up by a large proportion of the population even though smoking was thoroughly condemned by the imperial court. In 1639 the Chongzheng emperor (the last ruler of the Ming dynasty) published an imperial edict banning the sale of tobacco and threatening sellers with decapitation and exposure of their heads. It would seem that the emperor's decree was quite ineffective as he had to repeat it yearly until 1642. Berthold Laufer, an early writer on the introduction of tobacco into China, states that in 1641 the emperor lamented that his government could not enforce the prohibition because the princes and high officers smoked in private.

The use of snuff seems to have met with a much more favorable acceptance, probably because it was valued for its medicinal qualities. Snuff is produced by pulverizing dried tobacco leaves into a fine powder, usually with added herbs, spices, or other aromatic essences to enhance the flavor and fragrance. When sniffed up the nostrils, this compound produces a pleasant tingling sensation as well as a mild feeling of exhilaration as it clears congestion of the nasal passages by causing the user to sneeze. Like other forms of tobacco, snuff is highly addictive.

The Qing dynasty was established in 1644 when Manchu warriors from beyond the Great Wall swept down from the north to conquer China. The earliest known snuff bottles, made of bronze, belong to the first few years of the new reign. Sturdy, with simple incised decoration, dated, and inscribed with the name of their maker, Cheng Rongzhang, they would have been ideally suitable for use by the Tartar horsemen who accompanied the conquerors. While there has long been controversy regarding the authenticity of this group of early bottles, most leading authorities now believe that they are indeed genuine.

Writing in 1705, Wang Shizhen, a famous poet, literary critic, and statesman extraordinaire, stated:

> The country of Luzon [Philippines] produces a leaf for smoking called tobacco which is also known as "the gold-threaded fragrant leaf." When it arrives at the capital it is made into snuff which, it is said, can clear the eyes and, what is more, has the property of banishing infection. Glass bottles of all and every shape and color are made to contain it. The colors are red, purple, yellow, white, black and green; the white is like crystal and the red like fire. Things of great delight. There is an ivory spoon which is returned to the flask after snuffing. They are all manufactured within the Palace. Imitations are made by the common people but they never attain the standard of the original.[1]

At first confined to the elite of the new dynastic house, the popularity of snuff and snuff bottles was firmly established in and around the court at Beijing before the end of the seventeenth century. Several early references attest to the Kangxi emperor's own interest in the habit. In 1684, during one of his celebrated southern tours, the emperor visited Nanjing, and the Jesuit priest Ferdinand Verbiest noted in his *Authentic Records of the Kangxi Era* that the emperor, on being presented with various gifts by two other priests, issued the following decree:

> We have received your gifts. However, these items are rare nowadays even in your own country. We bestow you these items with the exception of snuff, the acceptance of which meets our approval.[2]

When Gao Shiqi retired from office in 1703, the emperor gave him one of his own snuff bottles as a retirement gift.[3] Another courtier, Wang Hao, escorted the emperor on a northern progress in the same year and recorded that he was given a glass bottle of snuff by the heir apparent.[4]

The Kangxi emperor reigned from 1662 to 1722 and, after restoring order in the transition from Ming to Manchu rule, became a patron of the arts. At some time in the 1680s, he established within the confines of the palace in Beijing a series of ateliers for the manufacture of works of art, including snuff bottles, for court use. The best craftsmen from all over China were brought to work there. One of the most important and most prolific of the imperial ateliers was the glassworks, established in 1696 under Jesuit supervision. Artists among the Jesuit missionaries also taught the Chinese European techniques of enameling on glass and on metalware.

The Kangxi emperor's deep interest in glasswares was continued during the succeeding Yongzheng and Qianlong reigns. The wide range of colors and styles already available to the glassmakers was particularly suited to the small size of the snuff bottle, and large numbers of these were produced within the imperial glassworks. It is recorded that in 1755, in addition to many other glass items, the Qianlong emperor ordered five hundred glass snuff bottles to be used as gifts at the summer palace at Chengde.[5]

Snuff taking appears to have remained a northern and imperial habit during most of the eighteenth century, and the use of snuff became a ritual of the upper classes. With such strong court patronage, it was inevitable that the snuff bottle should develop into an art form appreciated in its own right, rather than merely for its function. Beautiful, tactile, and so varied in style and material as to be endlessly fascinating, the minuscule containers upon which much art, taste, and money had been expended became the subject of active acquisition. The affluent formed inordinately large collections of these small but effective indicators of social status.

The Chinese habit of gift giving to ensure favorable treatment from official-dom found in these exquisite small objects an ideal means of making an opulent present in an unostentatious manner. Among the minority for whom money was considered demeaning as a form of exchange, snuff bottles thus became the currency of choice for the purchase of favors, positions, and advancement of one's political aims.

Encouraged by imperial usage, the snuff-taking habit spread slowly and gradually throughout China until, by 1800, snuff was used at every level of society throughout the vast Qing empire. For the next hundred years, the snuff bottle was a familiar sight in every home. It was a normal courtesy to offer friends a pinch of snuff upon meeting them in the street, and great status accrued to the owner of the finest or most unusual bottle. Indeed, the use of snuff and the collecting of snuff bottles had become such a veritable craze that, by the late 1830s, Sir John Francis Davis, in his book *The Chinese,* was moved to exclaim that "a Chinese is seldom seen without his snuff bottle."[6]

To supply the greatly increased demand, snuff bottles were manufactured in enormous quantities and in a much wider range of materials than previously. During the first part of the eighteenth century, glass, jade, and enameled wares constituted the majority of bottles made for the emperor and those connected with the court. By the end of the century, snuff bottles were being made in chalcedony, rock crystal, ivory, and lacquer. Still later, Chinese craftsmen displayed their skill and ingenuity by fashioning bottles from such exotic materials as amber, horn, coral, bamboo, mother-of-pearl, coconut, and tortoiseshell.

Although porcelain is virtually synonymous with China, and the great porcelain metropolis at Jingdezhen had been producing ceramic wares for the court for at least eight hundred years, porcelain snuff bottles apparently were not made there in any quantity until late in the Qianlong reign. Possibly the emperor saw no reason to order porcelain bottles from the distant south when outwardly similar and equally suitable enameled glass or metal bottles of higher quality could be produced more conveniently right in the palace workshops in Beijing. While the imperial collections in the National Palace Museum in Taipei include several superb matched sets of ten, twelve, or even twenty enameled porcelain bottles bearing Qianlong or Jiaqing marks, they do not compare in quality with the enameled glass bottles made in the palace workshops. Those early porcelain bottles were probably made as presentation pieces for visiting dignitaries.

Toward the end of the eighteenth century, however, the Jingdezhen kilns began to produce molded and carved porcelain snuff bottles, often in attempts to copy the various carved wares in other materials made at the palace workshops. The Jiaqing reign (1796–1820) saw a tremendous increase in the numbers of porcelain bottles created at Jingdezhen as the general populace took up the habit of snuff taking. While the better examples continued to be enameled, by far the vast majority were decorated in blue and white. During the remainder of the century, the snuff-taking habit reached the peak of its popularity with bottles being made of every available material and in every place where works of art were manufactured.

A most unusual innovation of the nineteenth century was the development of the inside-painted snuff bottle, with the decoration on the interior surface of a transparent material, usually clear, colorless glass or rock crystal, thus allowing the painting to show through. Using a narrow bamboo pen and working through the narrow opening that formed the mouth of the bottle, the artist painted his picture in reverse on the inside walls. The art of painting inside snuff bottles reached its peak in the late nineteenth and early twentieth century with the Beijing School. Zhou Leyuan, whose career spanned the period from 1881 to 1893, was the founder and master of this large school of painters.

The Chinese obsession with snuff and snuff bottles continued unabated throughout the nineteenth century and did not decline noticeably until the collapse of the Qing dynasty in 1911. The following forty years were so harsh and rigorous that all forms of art were totally forgotten in the struggle to survive.

Chinese snuff bottles, with their perfect combination of visual and tactile appeal, bear constant witness to the Chinese craftsman's aesthetic sensitivity and technical skill in turning a simple functional object into a treasured work of art. Today, both in China and in the West, these small masterpieces are finally regaining the serious recognition they so richly deserve.

During the 1970s I had the pleasure of meeting Stephen Thal, who with his wife has now donated their collection of snuff bottles to the Seattle Art Museum. At that time Stephen was working in his business, Fox's St. Francis, located at Union Square in the center of San Francisco. The Thal family was well known for creative, high-quality jewelry, and their discerning clientele included many celebrities.

While I am not sure exactly what sparked Stephen's interest in snuff bottles, I do know that his beginning was similar to that of many collectors in that he soon found his hobby difficult to sustain, and therefore he had to buy selectively and not as often as he would have liked. Stephen's experience in the jewelry business provided him with an ideal background for his love of snuff bottles, and his well-trained eyes made him an informed, critical judge of minerals and stones. He had an instinctive understanding of artistic design and was fully able to appreciate subtleties of form and natural markings. This discriminating taste is immediately evident in some outstanding examples in the collection of bottles he has donated to the Seattle Art Museum.

There is, for example, an extremely fine group of "silhouette" agates (cat. no. 16a–c). This term is used to designate those chalcedony bottles on which minimal surface carving, or even mere polishing, is used to bring out the design or pattern formed by the natural darker inclusions within the stone. These bottles required great skill on the part of the craftsman in choosing and cutting the material. The best of these bottles are extremely well hollowed so that natural light shining through the stone will emphasize the design.

An example illustrative of this technique is the chalcedony bottle (cat. no. 16a) depicting the deity Lan Caihe with a basket of flowers suspended over his shoulder while a monkey with a peach looks up and a bat hovers nearby. The three-character inscription, also carved from the darkly contrasting inclusion, reads: "A depiction of hundredfold longevity." The delicacy and skill with which the artist has used the natural material is exceptional.

Another silhouette agate worthy of special mention (cat. no. 16c) shows Liu Hai, the Daoist Immortal, holding his string of cash as he dances above his three-legged toad in what appears to be the entrance of a cave. The scene is dramatized by the carver's inspired use of the surrounding inclusion in the stone to frame the subject.

The Chinese carver's brilliant use of color is shown on a chalcedony bottle (cat. no. 13a) portraying two robust monkeys, each clasping a large peach while seated on a rocky ledge. This type of relief carving is sometimes known as cameo style, because the reddish "skin" or vein on the exterior of the bottle is carved as a cameo would be. This bold design is made even more powerful by the rich color of the inclusion and its contrast with the icy-looking, translucent background.

An exceptional carved porcelain bottle portraying a gnarled prunus tree (cat. no. 1) bears the mark of the potter Wang Bingrong. He was one of the few potters during the nineteenth century to emerge as an individual from among the traditionally anonymous craftsmen responsible for the mass production of ceramic wares at Jingdezhen. This small group of potters signed and dated their works and produced items mainly for the scholar class. They specialized in the carving of biscuit porcelain, which was then sometimes glazed with thin enamels in pastel colors. The body of this bottle is of a typical shape for this series, and while the basic shape was probably molded, the detail was always carved. This example, carved with strength and vigor, is one of Wang's masterpieces.

Among the glass bottles in the Thal collection, one that deserves particular attention is cat. no. 32, a pale bluish green overlay on a pink ground carved with double gourds growing on a vine. Overlay, or cased, glass was made by dipping the plain glass body into a vat of molten glass of a different color, thereby forming an outer layer or "skin." This outer layer was then carved back to the original surface, leaving the design standing in relief in the contrasting color. The color combination on this example is very rare and much sought after by collectors. The delicate design of this bottle is most attractive, and the gourd vine fills the available space naturally and without crowding. The foot of the bottle is formed by the lower bulbs of four of the gourds.

Another bottle worthy of note is cat. no. 29, a turquoise blue glass overlaid with opaque white. The carver exercised superb control to produce three writhing dragons, which fit easily, and yet with an air of tremendous vitality, into the small space available. The Chinese dragon is not the gruesome monster of medieval imagination, but a benign, good-natured creature and a cloud-dwelling bringer of life-giving rains. The dragon has been employed as a decorative element in China for thousands of years and is probably the Chinese motif most familiar to Westerners; it has thus become an enduring symbol of China itself.

Robert Hall
London

Notes

1. G. C. Tsang and Hugh M. Moss, *Snuff Bottles of the Ch'ing Dynasty,* exh. cat. (Hong Kong: Hong Kong Museum of Art, 1978), p. 28.

2. *Chinese Snuff Bottles,* exh. cat. (Hong Kong: Hong Kong Museum of Art, 1977), p. 16.

3. Ibid., p. 15.

4. Richard John Lynn, translation of the Zhao Zhiqian's "Yonglu Xianjie" (1868), *Journal of the International Chinese Snuff Bottle Society* 23, no. 3 (Autumn 1991), p. 10.

5. Yang Boda, "A Brief Account of Qing Dynasty Glass," in *Chinese Glass of the Qing Dynasty 1644–1911: The Robert H. Clague Collection* (Phoenix: Phoenix Art Museum, 1987).

6. Tsang and Moss, *Snuff Bottles of the Ch'ing Dynasty,* p. 34.

The Thal Collection of Chinese Snuff Bottles

FOR CENTURIES THE FLOWERING PLUM has inspired Chinese literati and artists through both its natural beauty and its symbolic meaning. The first plant to brave the frost and snow at the end of the winter with its elegant blossoms, the plum is praised as having "bones of jade, soul of ice," and it remains a favorite flower of the Chinese and in Chinese decorative arts.

The carver's keen sense of painting and sculpture is superbly demonstrated even within such a miniature scope. Freely wielding his iron "brush," his cutting tool, the artist not only lavished minute details of the motif but also created a convincing pictorial space. The huge, gnarled tree is filled with vitality, its branches clustered with luxuriant blossoms, and its branchlets, extending toward the infinite sky, accented with tightly closed buds. The incising is masterful, convincingly suggesting the rough bark and nodes of the tree and the filaments of the blossoms. The artist composed a scene that wraps around the bottle but ingeniously manipulated the pictorial vigor and rhythm by changing the visual impression from heavy and complicated on the front to light and sparse, verging on the infinite, at the back. The design imparts an air of delicate vibration, expressing wonderfully the purity and strength of the plum tree.

The artist, Wang Bingrong, was the foremost porcelain carver of the nineteenth century. Articles from his workshop were so outstanding that they were soon distinguished as from the Wang Bingrong School. His refined works range from objects for the scholar's studio to snuff bottles and possess a strong pictorial sense. Although the best-known subjects of his snuff bottles are the crane, the pine tree, and the dragon on a reticulated cloud ground, Wang excelled as well in other themes such as landscape and flowers and plants, as seen in the present example. The fine-grained white body and warm-toned glaze of this bottle successfully suggest the patina of ivory or jade carvings.

I   PORCELAIN SNUFF BOTTLE
19th century
By Wang Bingrong
H. 2⅞ in. (7.3 cm)
96.39.4

Of flattened pear shape, applied and carved with a continuous scene of a gnarled blossoming plum tree, covered with a cream-toned glaze, the base inscribed in relief Wang Bingrong zuo *(made by Wang Bingrong) in seal script, amethyst stopper.*

CATERING TO THE CHINESE FASHION for taking snuff in the eighteenth and nineteenth centuries, commercial kilns at Jingdezhen poured out large quantities of ceramic bottles for holding the powdered tobacco. Bottles of cylindrical shape covered with various glazes were popular over a sixty-year period from 1820 to 1880. The present bottle is among a small group that bear "motto" marks either enameled or inscribed at the base. In this case the motto (*shu,* meaning forgiveness) was meant to remind people to practice magnanimity toward their fellows in society.

The bird-and-flower motif has been one of the three major themes of Chinese painting since the tenth century (the other two are the landscape and the figure). Artists of the subject developed two distinctive styles. One is expressive, exploring the freedom of brush and ink; the other is refined, with richly colored and meticulous details. Cherished for both its splendid images and their symbolism, the latter style suited the palace taste particularly well, and it gradually became the dominant style in decorative arts, of which this bottle is a good example.

To successfully decorate a three-dimensional vessel, the artist must thoroughly exploit the particular surface he is given in order to create an illusion of space and animate imagery. In this case, the artist arranged the tree trunk diagonally across the cylindrical surface, thereby attracting the viewer to follow the tree and thus rotate the bottle. In doing so, the viewer is naturally led to see the whole design, which was superbly carved to occupy more than three-quarters of the surface.

2 PORCELAIN SNUFF BOTTLE
19th century
H. 2⅞ in. (7.3 cm)
96.39.3

Of cylindrical shape, molded in relief with a bird perching on a tree and two chrysanthemum flowers, details incised, covered with a pale blue glaze, the base with a raised character shu *(forgiveness), green glass stopper in the form of a flower bud.*

3 | PORCELAIN SNUFF BOTTLE
1796–1820
H. 2⅝ in. (6.7 cm)
96.39.2

Of oval shape resting on a ring foot, molded, carved in high relief and overglaze enameled in polychrome with an all-around design, on one side a boat carrying three people on a rolling wave, on the reverse five people holding objects and riding or standing by animals, above them swirling clouds in relief, the base with an iron-red reign mark reading Jiaqing nian zhi (made in the Jiaqing period, 1796–1820), imperial cap-shaped porcelain stopper in colors.

DUE TO THEIR SMALL SIZE, most porcelain snuff bottles were formed in molds rather than thrown on the potter's wheel; parts were then joined with a semi-liquid clay slip, and afterward glazed and fired.

Production of porcelain snuff bottles for the imperial court appears to have begun no later than the early eighteenth century at the imperial kilns at Jingdezhen, in Jiangxi province. But most were produced in the eighteenth and nineteenth centuries and largely decorated with *famille rose (fencai),* a style of overglaze enameling with a dominant rose-pink palette. Richly and exquisitely painted, such bottles imparted an imperial taste hardly matched by any other porcelain bottles. During the Qianlong and Jiaqing periods (1736–1820), they became one of the usual gifts bestowed by emperors to visiting dignitaries, particularly foreigners and honored Chinese military officials.[1] These bottles inevitably bear imperial reign marks.

During the Jiaqing period, porcelain bottles of organic forms or molded in high relief to imitate carved lacquer or ivory became popular. Their quantity increased vastly toward the mid-nineteenth century. The example seen here, molded in two parts, was joined with slip and a neck and foot added. After the joins were smoothed, the details of decoration were carved. The bottle was covered with a transparent glaze and fired into porcelain, then enameled and fired again, at a lower temperature, to fuse the enamels with the glazed surface.

The quality of a molded bottle depends primarily on the crispness of its shape and decoration, and on the refinement of its colors and painted designs. The molding of the present bottle is fine but not particularly sharp, and its simplified seal-script reign mark differs from the standard reign marks seen on both imperial snuff bottles and other imperial porcelain wares, suggesting that this bottle was an imitation made in a commercial kiln.[2]

Motifs such as the white elephant, exotic beasts and objects, and foreign figures identify the scene depicted here as "the eight barbarians bearing tributes" *(baman jinbao),* which promoted the idea that princes of other regions should pay annual respect and tributes to the Chinese emperor in exchange for his protection. The subject prevailed into the nineteenth century and often appeared on blue and white porcelain snuff bottles as well as polychrome enameled ones.[3]

detail
cat. no. 3

Notes

1. See the documents of the Qing court listed in Zhang, "A Study on the Manufacture of Snuff Bottles of the Qing Court," p. 18.

2. There is a group of molded porcelain bottles with such simplified reign marks; see, for example, Hui and Sin, *An Imperial Qing Tradition,* no. 30, and Sin et al., eds., *A Congregation of Snuff Bottle Connoisseurs,* no. 117. A bottle in the Seattle Art Museum collection (SAM 33.886) is of similar size and decoration but is slightly more almond-shaped and with a finer execution in molding and painting. Its red, standard four-character seal mark matches exactly those of imperial porcelain vessels; see Fuller, *Chinese Snuff Bottles in the Seattle Art Museum,* 1970, no. 63, left. Porcelain snuff bottles with the standard four-character Jiaqing reign mark in seal script can be found in Zhang, ed., *Snuff Bottles in the Collection of the National Palace Museum,* nos. 78, 83–95.

3. One exquisite blue and white example can be seen in Fuller, *Chinese Snuff Bottles in the Seattle Art Museum,* no. 64, upper right.

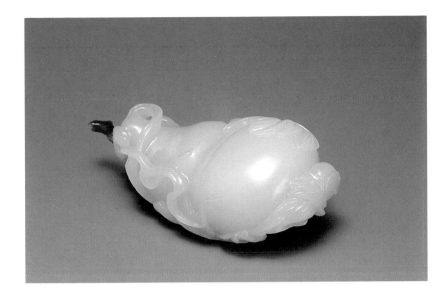

4 | NEPHRITE SNUFF BOTTLE
19th century
H. 2¾ in. (7 cm)
96.39.45

Of even white, carved in the form of a double gourd contoured by sprawling leafy vines and tendrils which bear a baby double-gourd at the bottom, stem-shaped glass stopper in coral red.

JADE, KNOWN AS *yu* IN CHINESE, is a synonym for two distinct minerals, jadeite and nephrite. For thousands of years, Chinese artisans carved primarily nephrite, which was more readily accessible. Composed of tremolite and acti-nolite (both silicates of calcium and magnesium), nephrite belongs to the am-phibole group of minerals. It occurs in several colors, but in its pure state, it is white and generally preferred. One of the largest nephrite deposits is in the region of the Central Asia cities of Khotan and Yarkand, in today's Xinjiang Autonomous Region in western China.[1] At first the mineral was gathered in the pebbles and boulders naturally washed out by two famous rivers, the so-called white and black jade rivers, which flow from the Kunlun Mountains. In the late sixteenth century, mining started.

The slightly depressed planes seen on both sides of this gourd bottle pre-serve the true shape of the natural pebble from which it is made. These con-tours may be less realistic than a real gourd, but they are the perfect marks of an artistic approach that wasted nothing of a precious raw material. The design is intended to conjure up the gourd form as completely as possible from the original shape of the stone. The trailing leafy vines, reticulated at the tip of the gourd, spread along both sides and end with a baby gourd at the bottom. The ingenuity of the design, the meticulous attention to detail, and the smooth, unctuous feel of the jade make this bottle an exquisite work of art.

There is an old saying in China: if all the seeds of a gourd are sowed, the next year will bring one hundred gourds. Thus the gourd has long been a symbol for a hundred sons and grandsons. A combination of large and small double gourds with sprawling vines forms two very auspicious rebuses: "may you have numerous descendants" *(guadi mianmian)* and "may sons and grandsons continue for ten thousand generations" *(zisun wandai)*. The subject is a time-honored favorite in Chinese decorative arts, and was preferred particularly by the emperor Qianlong (1736–95).[2] Snuff bottles of such designs are often the finest in material and carving, as attested by a group of jade bottles now in the palace museums in Beijing and Taipei.[3]

Notes

1. James Watt, *Chinese Jades from the Collection of the Seattle Art Museum* (Seattle: Seattle Art Museum, 1989), pp. 15–16.

2. For an exquisite ivory box and stand in the form of a gourd dating from the Qianlong reign, see Wen C. Fong and James Watt, *Possessing the Past: Treasures from the National Palace Museum, Taipei* (New York: Metropolitan Museum of Art, 1996), pl. 327.

3. See Xia, ed., *Masterpieces of Snuff Bottles in the Palace Museum*, nos. 121, 129, and Zhang, ed., *Snuff Bottles in the Collection of the National Palace Museum*, nos. 138, 142–43, 145–47, 227.

5 | NEPHRITE SNUFF BOTTLE
1750–1850
H. 2¼ in. (5.7 cm)
96.39.47

Of white nephrite, carved to depict a crouching rabbit with paws tucked underneath and ears laid back, attached to its mouth a stemlike red glass stopper with green glass collar.

THE CHINESE HAVE PREFERRED JADE (technically nephrite) as a gemstone for nearly six thousand years. So hard (about 6.5 on the Mohs scale) that it could not be cut directly by any metal tools, ancient craftsmen resorted to the force of abrasion to grind it down. The usual abrasive was quartz sand, aided by water. During the Qing dynasty, jade was shaped and drilled with diamond-tipped tools, but still in conjunction with abrasives.

The shape of this rabbit was patiently worked out by abrasion, a process requiring an intensity of labor and an amount of time now hard to imagine. To hollow out the bottle's interior, the carver first drilled a cylindrical shaft, using a steel tube (substituting for the bamboo tube of the past) to carry the abrasives. The diameter of this tube determined the size of the bottle's mouth. After that, a flat, crooked metal tool loaded with abrasives enlarged the shaft to achieve the thin wall of the bottle.

Jade is appreciated for its translucency and oily surface, which is always carefully polished to impart a wonderful sense of warmth and tactility. Its rarity and the enormous labor invested in working it made jade a symbol of wealth as well as prestige. A rabbit-shaped bottle is both a sculpture and a utensil, perfect for visual appreciation as well as handling.

JADE IS ONE OF THE EARLIEST MEDIA employed for artistic expression, and artifacts made from it are highly cherished in China. As early as the fourth millennium B.C., objects worked from jade played a part in rituals and ceremonies. Large quantities of burial jades found in tombs dating before 3000 B.C. attest to the ancient Chinese belief that the stone possessed a protective and preservative power. Like the jade pigs held by the deceased in each hand, the jade cicada, placed in the mouth, was a popular burial jade in the Eastern Han period (25–220).

By the seventh century, however, ornamental jade as trinkets had become popular, reflecting a change in attitude toward the material in late imperial China. Although many traditional motifs are retained in later jade designs, the themes became more decorative and their meanings more temporal. The present cicada is such a case: it played no ritual role and evoked no more than a worldly wish for immortality, honesty, and integrity.[1] A trend toward snuff bottles in formalized animal shapes developed during the late eighteenth and nineteenth centuries, and many cicada-shaped snuff bottles survive today.

Notes
1. The cicada is a symbol of rebirth to the Chinese because of its life cycle. Spending the first thirteen to fourteen years of its life underground, it only surfaces in its final larval state, shedding its case, and becoming fully formed. In legend it was believed that the cicada fed on dew and did not otherwise eat, thus freeing it from corruption. Odes to cicada written by famous Tang poets are well known and still recited with enthusiasm.

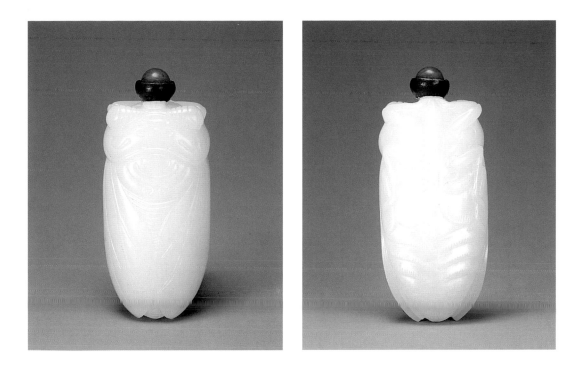

6 | NEPHRITE SNUFF BOTTLE
19th century
H. 2⅝ in. (6.7 cm)
96.39.46

Of white nephrite, carved in the form of a cicada, with descriptive lines for veins of the transparent wings and for eyes and body features, the underside with detailed carapace and six folded legs, coral stopper with silver collar.

Of a white pebble suffused with beautiful russet inclusions, glass stopper and collar imitating orange chalcedony and green jade.

THE VARIED COLORS OF NEPHRITE come from the metallic irons found in the matrix of the stone, the most common being the ferrous irons that give rise to shades of light to dark green, and the ferric irons that result in yellow to reddish brown shades, as seen on the present example.[1] Naturally shaped and polished by river flows, the pebble nephrite has an irregular form, smooth texture, and naturally gradational color, all tastefully preserved and presented in this bottle. By retaining the natural form, the bottle imparts a deceptively rustic flavor to a practical luxury.

Notes
1. James Watt, *Chinese Jades from the Collection of the Seattle Art Museum* (Seattle: Seattle Art Museum, 1989), p. 16.

NEPHRITE SNUFF BOTTLE
18th–19th century
H. 2¹⁄₁₆ in. (5.2 cm)
96.39.42

Of white with light brown inclusions on one side, flattened rectangular form with rounded shoulders, carved through the light brown skin with a chi *dragon over a raised rectangular panel, a plain reverse and an agate stopper with a black vinyl collar.*

THE *chi* IS A HORNLESS DRAGON whose long snakelike tail splits at the tip into two spirals. Legend has it that the emperor Wu (156–87 B.C.) of the Western Han dynasty reportedly left his palace one night for a secret inspection of the capital city, only to find a *chi* dragon wandering in the street.[1] This and other legends imply that the *chi,* like other dragons, is related to royalty. The image of the *chi* was a favorite motif in imperial designs, although its use was not limited to such objects. The earliest known form of the *chi* dragon appears on bronze vessels of the eighth century B.C., and in the late sixteenth century the motif became popular on artworks of varied media, but was most frequently rendered as a sculptural element on ceramic vessels and jade works.[2] During the eighteenth century the *chi* dragon was a staple motif on snuff bottles produced by imperial and commercial workshops alike, with commercial bottles often copying imperial ones.[3]

Although confined by a flat, tiny rectangular panel, the carver of this bottle succeeded in creating a seemingly large pictorial space around the *chi* dragon.

Its imposing strength is expressed through a round, masculine body, and its powerful, agile movement—descending from the top and moving from back to front—evokes a sense of three-dimensional space. The fluid lines and the bulging muscles of the dragon's body establish the design as both a two-dimensional picture and as a three-dimensional sculpture.

Notes

1. Wang Qi and Wang Siyi, *Illustrated Compendium of the Three Powers* (Sancai Tuhui), vol. Bird and Animal 5, no. 5, reprinted by Shanghai Ancient Books (Shanghai Guji Chubanshe), 1988.

2. A Dehua teapot decorated with *chi* dragon appliqué is now in the National Palace Museum, Taipei; see Wen C. Fong and James Watt, *Possessing the Past: Treasures from the National Palace Museum, Taipei* (New York: Metropolitan Museum of Art, 1996), pl. 252; related vessels, a teapot (B60P2390) and a vase (B60P1323), can also be seen in the collection of the Asian Art Museum of San Francisco.

3. Moss et al., *A Treasury of Chinese Snuff Bottles,* vol. Jade, p. 243.

9 | NEPHRITE SNUFF BOTTLE
1740–1850
H. 2¹¹⁄₁₆ in. (6.8 cm)
96.39.44

Of pure yellowish green with dark gradational brown skin on one side, flattened rectangular form resting on a neat-cut ring foot, carved animal masks with rings on both shoulders, the front carved through the brown skin with a landscape of a rocky mountain in which a towering pine tree grows over a scholar and fisherman sitting on opposite sides of a stream, and a farmer on a buffalo and a woodcutter carrying a bundle of firewood walk on the mountain path above, a small brown inclusion at the mouth, reverse side plain, coral stopper with a gilt silver collar.

THIS BOTTLE IS A CLASSIC EXAMPLE of the Master of the Rocks School.[1] Its pure, yellowish green color is superb, forming a strong contrast with the natural dark brown skin. The inside is well hollowed and particularly remarkable for the fact that the hollowing was done through an unusually small mouth. The animal masks on the shoulders and their slightly elongated oval rings are also well fashioned. The crisp carving of an extremely detailed design within a confined space indicates a masterful control of the medium.[2]

The subject of the design, the so-called four noble occupations, is a favored one for this school. The figure sitting under the pine tree, a scholar, holds an open book in his hand as he gazes into the distance, as if in meditation.

Opposite him, on the other side of the flowing stream, a fisherman is identified by his fishing rod and basket. The occupations of farmer and woodcutter are also clearly indicated by their attributes, respectively, a buffalo and a bundle of firewood. Together the four occupations represent the theme of eremitism, or religious seclusion, a cherished lifestyle among scholar-officials. The reader sharpens his intellectual power, the fisherman detaches himself from the pollution of politics, and the farmer and woodcutter avoid material luxuries. In all, the practitioner achieves harmony with the grand nature, such a harmony being the embodiment of the Way *(dao)*, the fundamental principle by which the world is sustained.

The scholarly subject and the masterful treatment of the contrasting natural colors of the jade connect this bottle to the carvers of the Suzhou School. Suzhou, a town south of the Changjiang (or Yangtze) River and near the Da Yunhe (or Grand Canal, an ancient manmade waterway), was a main center for hardstone carving which flourished from the seventeenth to the early twentieth centuries. Commercial jade carvers produced objects of new types for a market of affluent merchants and city dwellers. Incorporating naturalistic elements in their designs of landscapes and flora and fauna, they achieved a pictorial style distinguished in both its motifs and technique. One unique characteristic of the Suzhou School is the use of the outer skin or inclusions to form or highlight the design, not only to achieve artistic value but to minimize waste. The concept of transforming natural flaws into integral elements of a design, called "ingenious making" *(qiaodiao* or *qiaozuo)*, was brilliant and highly appreciated throughout generations (see cat. no. 12 for an example). This approach was similar to that utilized by the Master of the Rocks School, but its designs relied on forming a relief panel from the whole layer of skin.

In the present example, the lines are superbly carved or incised to describe forms and to layer pictorial depth. Although parts of the surface have been worn from use, many details are still clear and lively, such as the folds of clothes, the woven patterns of the fishing basket, the rough textures of the pine tree and rocks, and the rivulets of the flowing stream. It is also worth noting that visual contrasts play a significant role in the design. The differences between dark brown and pure, light yellowish green, between the matte, rough skin and the smooth, clear body, and between the complicated foreground carving and the plain background add much to the vividness of the design.

detail
cat. no. 9

Notes

1. The term was coined by the authors (Moss et al.) of *A Treasury of Chinese Snuff Bottles,* vol. Jade. It applies only to a group of jade snuff bottles whose carving equals the quality of the better-known Suzhou wares. The authors think that this school possibly represents an alternative Suzhou style. These bottles, often of rectangular form, can be dated from 1740 to 1850. They are usually of yellowish green nephrite with a dark brown skin through which a design in low, detailed relief is carved, with distinctive animal masks with rings on both shoulders. See ibid., pp. 340–73.

2. For related examples, see Moss et al., *A Treasury of Chinese Snuff Bottles,* nos. 134–43, and Sin et al., eds., *A Congregation of Snuff Bottle Connoisseurs,* nos. 172–74.

THE GOD OF LONGEVITY, SHOULAO, appears as a slim old man with a long white beard and an elongated, bald head with a bump at the forehead. A stellar god, he lives in a palace at the south pole and is often seen holding or being presented with a peach, the emblem of life. In Chinese cosmology the south is the region of life. The double gourd, a typical item in the Daoist's paraphernalia, is considered a miniature replica of heaven and earth, uniting the two in one shape. When the gourd is opened, it releases a cloud which can be used to trap demons. The bat is a symbol of good luck and happiness, as the pronunciation of "bat" *(fu)* is identical in sound with the word for "good fortune" *(fu)*. The pictorial motifs of the design thus make an auspicious pun, "double happiness of fortune and longevity," which is inscribed in four characters on the reverse of the bottle. The Chinese found pictorial puns and rebuses hugely appealing, and they prevailed in the designs of decorative arts of the Ming and Qing periods, particularly in the eighteenth century and later. They usually expressed wishes for worldly success.

The lines on this bottle were skillfully carved, clearly defining varied forms such as the undulating smoke or clouds, the folds of clothing, facial features, and the texture of the garden rocks. The russet inclusions, however, were retained not for artistic purposes as the color has no bearing on the pictured scene, but from the commercial necessity to retain as much of the raw jade as possible. During the late eighteenth century, jade works were so sought after that sometimes they were sold less by their workmanship than by the weight and quality of the stone.

10 | NEPHRITE SNUFF BOTTLE
Early 19th century
H. 2½ in. (6.8 cm)
96.39.43

*Of mottled dark gray suffused with gradational russet on one side,
flattened rectangular form, carved in relief through the russet inclusions
with a rockery scene in which a monkey presents a peach to Shoulao
(god of longevity) who holds a staff with his left hand and on his back
carries a double gourd, from which escapes a bat and smoke, which
forms clouds above, the reverse side carved in relief in seal script with
four characters* fushou shuangquan *(double happiness of fortune and
longevity), coral stopper with a black vinyl collar.*

11 | JADEITE SNUFF BOTTLE
Early 19th century
H. 2¼ in. (5.7 cm)
96.39.50

Of snow white with emerald green inclusions, flattened rectangular shape on a ring foot, tourmaline stopper with silver collar, a minor crack on one shoulder.

UNLIKE NEPHRITE, TO WHICH CHINESE CRAFTSMEN had early access, jadeite *(feicui)* did not come into use in China until the seventeenth century, when it was imported from northern Burma (Myanmar). Although listed with nephrite in the category of jade, jadeite is in fact a different material, being a silicate of sodium and aluminum and therefore belonging to the pyroxene mineral group. In its purest state, it is white and appears translucent. Like nephrite, jadeite (6.5 to 7 degrees on the Mohs scale) is an exceptionally tough material and resists efforts to break it.

Jadeite snuff bottles of the late eighteenth and the early nineteenth centuries have no carved decoration, an artistic plainness that is meant to focus attention on the intrinsic character of the material. The green inclusions that naturally occur in the translucent surface form a beautiful contrast with the crystallized snow-white color. The elegant design and the cool smoothness of the material invite the touch of both the eye and the hand.

*Of pale honey tone with black inclusions, flattened oval shape with
a flat oval base, incised, carved, and undercut in relief with a design
continuing on both sides, on the front a scene of three figures playing
in a rock garden with black inclusions reserved for clothes, firecrackers,
musical stone, and pine needles, on the reverse a courtyard enclosed by
a zigzag wall with a door and rows of lattice windows, a plum tree
with flower buds reserved in tiny black inclusions, ribbonlike clouds
above, tourmaline stopper with a black vinyl collar.*

CHALCEDONY IS A FINE-GRAINED (cryptocrystalline) type of quartz. It is a
stone of clear, translucent tones with or without a dark skin or inclusions. Because of variations in its color and texture, it is known by many other names.
One is "agate," for a variety with concentric bands; another is "dendritic chalcedony" or "moss agate," for a kind with fernlike inclusions. As an inexpensive
semiprecious stone, chalcedony was used extensively in snuff bottle production
during the nineteenth century.

Judging by its style, this bottle can be attributed to the famous Suzhou
School, which was named for a small town south of the Changjiang (or
Yangtze) River and near the Da Yunhe (Grand Canal) in today's Jiangsu prov-
ince. Since the late sixteenth century, Suzhou has been renowned for its

hardstone carvings. Whether small trinkets or snuff bottles, the conspicuous characteristics of this school are the ingenious use of every natural color in the material to form decorative elements in the overall design and the skillful undercutting of recessed planes and rock work to create pictorial perspective. The finish of the objects is always exquisite, their surfaces carefully polished to erase any trace of tool marks and to bring out a sheen. Snuff bottles of this style are highly valued and were eagerly sought even at the time of their production.

The subject of this bottle is a scene of the Chinese Spring Festival, indicated by the pine tree and plum blossoms and the children who playfully carry auspicious objects and light firecrackers. The composition is obviously adapted to the black natural inclusions in the material. Although the design continues around the entire bottle, it is partitioned by a superb rock work located at the right front edge that extends to the reverse. Such rock work is typical in the construction of actual gardens at Suzhou. As indispensable decorative elements these garden rocks are enjoyed not only for their unique appearance but also for their special significance in building the views and moods of a garden. They can be cleverly integrated into garden structure as steps, stairs, or part of a wall, and it is from this practical use that the carver of this bottle must have drawn inspiration, for the rock on the reverse plays just such a role.

The designer of the bottle created a strong sense of perspective by carving and undercutting a number of pictorial planes. These planes not only indicate and broaden pictorial distance and illusionary space but also function as formal elements. The sculptural form of the rock work, for example, is wonderfully suggested by the undercutting of the stone into tiered and serrated planes.

The masterful incorporation of natural inclusions is a fundamental technique of the Suzhou School and in many cases was the starting point for a design. In the present example, every inclusion was exploited to form and emphasize motifs. Thick layers of black depict the clothes of the larger figure and the pine needles, while thinner layers varying in tone from black to brown delineate the firecrackers, a *qing* (a musical stone), the clothes of two small figures, and on the reverse, flower buds. The inclusions dramatically contrast with the forms carved on the clear surfaces such as the figures' faces and the background settings. The composition on the front, centered on a large patch of inclusions, has a heavier visual weight and a busier nature, which is conveyed largely through carving in varying depths. The reverse, by comparison, bears only two small inclusions, and the design shifts to a lighter tone that is expressed in the lack of human figures and by the use of shallower undercutting and incising. The design on the bottle thus has two pictorial moods: one lively with human excitement and celebrating, the other tranquil with plants and clouds flowing in a moderate breeze. Moreover, with the skillfully located rock work acting as intermediary, the contrasting moods appear not arbitrary but compensatory and integral. A cloud in the shape of a *ruyi* head is incised on the neck of the bottle and indicates the common Suzhou School practice of including every part of the surface in the carved design.

Two propitious greetings frequently used in the Spring Festival are incorporated into the design as rebuses. The first, "peace is called in by the explosion of firecrackers" *(zubao pingan)* is formed by the image of the larger figure wearing an official cap who bends down to light some firecrackers as a cute little child at the left watches attentively while nervously covering his ears. Another child holds a *ruyi,* a symbol of good luck, with its ribbons fastened to a musical stone, symbolizing "auspiciousness, happiness, and as you wish" *(jiqing ruyi).*

Both bottles of flattened circular shape resting on a ring foot.

(a) *The smaller bottle of translucent white with red skin, carved in high relief with a continuous rockery setting, on the front two monkeys reserved in red each hold a peach and on the reverse one monkey holds a peach, red agate stopper with silver collar.*

(b) *The larger bottle of pale honey tone with black inclusions, on one side three monkeys carved in relief within the black inclusions, on the other side a depression in the stone transformed into the mouth of a spring from which water flows into a rockery, well hollowed, jadeite stopper with black vinyl collar.*

IN THESE TWO BOTTLES the use of contrasting colors to form designs and create dramatic effect is obviously after the style of the Suzhou School, as is the choice of motifs such as rock work and animals. The carving is not as excellent as the previous example, however. On the smaller bottle, the relief is a little too high, and on the larger bottle the undercutting is not sophisticated enough to form serrated rock work. Their designs are nevertheless quite original, with a naturalistic rendering of the monkeys, every one of which is individualized. The carving and incising of facial features and fur are detailed and descriptive. The tiny depression on the larger bottle is cleverly transformed into the mouth of a spring.

In the seventeenth century, the makers of Chinese decorative arts began to incorporate auspicious signs into their designs. The cute appearance and appealing characteristics of the monkey certainly make it a favorite motif, but its popularity is also related to its symbolic meanings. A popular god known in every household is the monkey king, Sun Wukong. In the fourteenth-century novel, *The Journey to the West* (Xiyou Ji), he accompanied the Buddhist pilgrim Xuanzang of the Tang period (618–907) to India and protected him from myriad dangers. He was therefore revered and worshiped as "the great saint equal to heaven" *(qitian dasheng)*. A monkey holding a peach symbolizes best wishes for longevity. According to legend, in the orchard of the Queen Mother of the West (Xiwangmu), peaches came to fruition only once every three thousand years, and they guaranteed immortality to whomever might eat one. But the monkey king once stole and ate them all.

CHALCEDONY SNUFF
BOTTLE
Late 18th–19th century
H. 2⁵⁄₁₆ in. (5.9 cm)
96.39.10

Of translucent, clear tones with mottled brown inclusions, circular shape resting on a ring foot, on the front a monkey reserved in brown and, carved in low relief, riding on a horse with a bee flying ahead, on the reverse an incised bee at the bottom, well hollowed, orange-toned quartz stopper with a glass bead finial in pearl color and a gilt silver collar.

HOW WELL THE NATURAL INCLUSIONS in the stone were transformed into elements of a design is always important in judging the quality of a bottle of this kind. The design of this bottle is clever. The large black patches are turned into mottling on the monkey's skin, while a small dotty inclusion on the right forms the eyes of a flying bee. The carving and incising are succinct and sketchy, with the monkey, horse, and bees all outlined, like drawings. The bottle is well hollowed, bringing out the fine translucency of the stone.

The Chinese word for monkey *(hou),* has the same pronunciation as the word for "marquis"; similarly, the pronunciation of bee *(feng)* is identical to the verb "to confer." A monkey on a horse with bees flying ahead thus forms the popular rebus "may you be immediately conferred with the rank of marquis" *(mashang fenghou),* a wish for promotion to a higher rank or office.

15 | AGATE SNUFF BOTTLE
19th century
H. 2¼ in. (5.7 cm)
96.39.9

Of light honey tones with brown and ocher striated inclusions and mottled ocher and russet skins, flattened rectangular shape resting on a ring foot, carved through the ocher skin on one side with a man holding a triangular banner on a horse, the reverse reserved in beige and russet with two monkeys one on top of the other, and a bee incised on one shoulder, tiger's-eye stopper with light green glass collar.

THE AESTHETIC APPROACH OF THE SUZHOU SCHOOL, in which raw materials are fully exploited, is seen again on this example. Decorative motifs are not only skillfully formed within the confines of the natural skins but also singled out in relief for emphasis. Mottled ocher skin adds an interesting effect to the spotty horse and to the seemingly worn-out banner, while the beige and russet skin gives a lifelike impression to the monkey's fur.

The motif of a man on horseback holding a fluttering banner makes a rebus meaning "may you win the victory the moment you raise your standard" *(qikai desheng),* expressing a wish for speedy success. Monkeys seen one on top of the other and together with a bee form the rebus "may generation after generation be bestowed with the rank of marquis" *(beibei fenghou).*

16 THREE CHALCEDONY
SNUFF BOTTLES
Late 18th–19th century
H. *(a)* 1¹⁵⁄₁₆ in. (4.9 cm),
(b) 2⅜ in. (6 cm),
(c) 2⅝ in. (6.7 cm)
(a) 96.39.11, *(b)* 96.39.12,
(c) 96.39.13

(a) *Chalcedony, of translucent pale beige tones with black inclusions on one side, small flattened rectangular shape resting on a ring foot, lightly carved on the inclusion with a deity carrying a basket followed by a monkey holding a peach, all riding on clouds, and a bat flying behind, three characters* baishou tu *(a picture celebrating hundredfold longevity) on the top, plain reverse, jadeite stopper with silver collar.*

(b) *Agate, of pale honey tones with inclusions ranging from dark brown to black, flattened rounded square shape resting on a large ring foot, lightly carved in some dark patches on the front with a man and a bird, the bird's head turning toward the man, the reverse with white and small dark inclusions, jadeite stopper with silver collar.*

(c) *Agate, of light brown tones with dark brown striated and patch inclusions, flattened rounded square shape resting on a large ring foot, lightly carved in the dark patch on the front with a figure wielding a ribbon strung with coins and stepping on a three-legged toad, plain reverse, coral-colored glass stopper with enameled silver collar.*

THIS TYPE OF CHALCEDONY OR AGATE is commonly known as "silhouette" or "shadow" agate, for the dark inclusions of stone are usually outlined and incised to form such a low relief that the motifs appear more like flat paper-cut patterns attached to the stone than three-dimensional sculptural carvings. Unlike the previous examples (cat. nos. 12–15), in which motifs stand out in reliefs with the backgrounds cut away, silhouette images seem to sink into the stone, their design delineated by cutting and incising the dark inclusions. The former technique suggests a sculpture on stone while the latter evokes a painting on the stone surface. Silhouette images are usually less detailed and suggested largely by simple outline.

It is unusual to find such a clear picture as on the bottle at the left. All the motifs, particularly the three characters, are presented with absolute clarity even though the design itself is of miniature scale. It is also surprising to find a silhouette image as lively and with such a strong sense of movement as that on the bottle at the right. Although still depending on simple outlines, the carver masterfully used curvilinear forms to create dynamic movement. As the figure jumps on the toad, his hip turns and his garment blows full in the wind. He wields the ribbon with such effort and speed that it flutters and waves into an arabesque. One can almost hear the jingling sound of the coins. The figure is depicted in mid-jump, his legs drawn up and further intensifying the sense of movement. A large circular band of natural striated inclusions frames the image.

The middle bottle represents a new aesthetic approach in design. Inspired by the darker inclusions of stone, the carver composed the image by following their shapes as closely as possible with a minimum of carving. Instead of transforming all the dark inclusions into organic forms, the carver left some untouched, allowing them to naturally form part of the image or to serve as settings for the image. On this bottle, cutting was limited to the facial features of the man and the bird; their bodies take their form from the natural inclusions alone. Such an approach creates marvelous visual effects quite similar to those of splashed-ink paintings.

The subject represented on the middle bottle is ambiguous in its meaning, but that of the bottle on the right is widely known as "Liu Hai toying with the toad" (Liu Hai xichan), a theme that prevailed in both Chinese painting and decorative arts. Liu Hai, abandoning worldly wealth to become a true Daoist, is revered as a benevolent deity. The image of him wielding the string of coins is a symbol for bestowing wealth. The figure depicted on the bottle at the left

is Lan Caihe, one of the Eight Immortals, whose emblem is a flower or fruit basket. He is obviously on the way to the Peach Festival, a festivity for the gods given by the Queen Mother of the West to celebrate longevity. The monkey and the bat are indicative of longevity as well. The auspicious subject thus makes this bottle an ideal birthday gift.

Of pale honey tones with striated inclusions on both sides ranging from light brown to black, rounded square shape resting on a large broad ring foot, on the front thriftily outlined in the dark patches a bird perching on a branch with its head turning back to look at the moon, mottled reverse, well hollowed, lapis lazuli stopper with tiger's-eye collar.

THE STRIATED INCLUSIONS OF THE NATURAL STONE are here superbly integrated into the overall design. They serve as leaves and branches of the tree on which the bird perches and as the rock cliffs next to which the moon rises. The succinct forms of the lightly touched motifs and the striations evoke the expressive brushstrokes of Chinese ink painting, while the natural color grada tions and the interesting halos around the moon and bird resemble marvelously emotional ink washes. By casting fuzzy images and moonlit shadows into the composition, the designer achieved an unusually romantic night scene.

The subject of a single bird, with its distinctively large body and beak suggesting an eagle, is quite familiar to the Chinese audience. As a symbol of strength, the eagle is often depicted standing alone either on a pine tree or on a rock in the sea, "the hero who fights alone" *(yingxiong duli)*. Objects decorated with such a motif are an appropriate gift for an elderly man, wishing him the strength of the eagle and the longevity of the pine.

18 │ AGATE SNUFF BOTTLE
1750–1860
H. 2⁵⁄₁₆ in. (5.8 cm)
96.39.15

Of pale creamy tones with light to dark brown inclusions on both sides, flattened rectangular shape with a slightly indented oval base, on the front with natural striations and "cotton wool" patterns, very well hollowed, amethyst stopper with silver collar.

BY SIMPLY USING THE NATURAL INCLUSIONS of the stone as its decorative subject, the carver of this bottle raised the enjoyment of it to a new aesthetic level. Instead of responding to a specific, well-defined motif, the viewer is left to conjure his or her own imaginative picture from the natural shades and shapes or to appreciate them as pure abstractions.

The bottle is extremely well hollowed and its exterior carefully polished, further enhancing its translucency. Yet the interior wall is left unpolished, perhaps deliberately so, to show a web of large tool marks reminiscent of cloud clusters. These clusters not only echo the natural form of the colored inclusions but also provide a wonderful setting for them. They create a sense of lightness in which the light brown "cotton wool" motifs appear to float on the surface.

Of pale honey tones with striated inclusions ranging from light ocher to black on both sides, flattened pear shape on an indented oval base, extremely well hollowed, coral stopper with black vinyl collar.

THE DESIGN OF THIS BOTTLE is composed entirely of unaltered natural, abstract forms which are strikingly beautiful in their own right. Rather than transform the natural lines and colors into formal elements representative of the objective world, the carver chose them precisely for their subjective and expressive characteristics. Such a conception is almost modern in essence and coincides with the temperament of modern art in the West.

The bottle is extremely well hollowed and polished to a very thin wall, resulting in an almost transparent surface. The rugged shape of the central loop of dark inclusion suggests a metal band or a rigid rock work, while the remaining inclusions resemble traces of freely executed brushstrokes and ink washes. The varied color gradations, whether in dots, patches, or lines, further increase the charm of the natural forms. An intriguing aspect of the bottle is that when viewed against a light, the design changes. Because the wall is so thin and transparent, the patterns on both sides visually juxtapose and mingle with each other, resulting in more fascinating effects. On the reverse, for example, an ocher dot in the shape of a kidney bean appears to float, haloed by the outline of the dark loop on the front.

*Of light brown with dark brown inclusions and opaque buff skin
around the mouth, in the shape of a Chinese date, the skin carved
in the form of a peanut husk, stem-shaped coral stopper.*

THE DESIGN OF THIS BOTTLE is related to a group of chalcedony snuff bottles, all in the form of a Chinese date to which one or several peanut husks is attached. They have thus won the nickname of "peanut agate." Unlike other examples, however, in which the realistic depiction of the peanut husk is paramount, the carver of this bottle emphasized the realism of the date. Not only did he patiently carve dozens of thin intaglio lines to depict the unique surface of a special type of date, he also cleverly utilized existing patches of dark inclusions to suggest bruised spots on the fruit. Particularly remarkable is the round spot in the lower front side, where the slightly depressed surface conveys a sense of softness. What a humorous and delightful touch!

The combination of a date with peanut husks, two unrelated motifs, stems purely from the symbolic meaning that together they convey. Borrowing one word from each motif forms the rebus "may you quickly get precious sons" *(zaosheng guizi)*. Bottles like this were therefore suitable wedding gifts.

*Of dense dark green with dark red skin on one side and ocher striated
inclusions on the other, flattened rectangular shape resting on a ring
foot, carved in relief on both sides, on the front with a woman poling
a raft on which sits an old man reserved in the red skin, a bird above
in flight, on the reverse with the two deities He and He on a large
banana leaf, and a bird flying above, coral-colored glass stopper with
a hole for a now missing finial.*

ALTHOUGH BELONGING TO THE QUARTZ FAMILY, jasper differs from the rest of
its members in that it is completely opaque. The visual appeal of a jasper snuff
bottle lies not only in its carved decoration but in the density and strong colors
of the stone itself. Jasper is usually dark green, russet, or ocher. Sometimes it
has a skin or striated inclusions of similar tones.

This bottle is decorated in a uniquely bold and vigorous style that accords
well with the dense and heavy quality of the stone. The figures and objects are
carved in relief in simple lines and large planes, producing rounded forms that
readily imply resilient flesh and muscles. This style is particularly successful in
depicting the two boys, whose full, fleshy cheeks and chubby bodies beneath
their garments are convincingly suggested.

Images of deities are favorite subjects in Chinese decorative art. The Chinese believe that paying tributes to the gods enables one's wishes to be realized.
The two rotund boys with shoulder-length hair are, in fact, the Heavenly Twins

He and He. One god is usually portrayed holding a lotus and the other, a box containing precious and propitious objects. "Lotus" and "box," both *he* in Chinese, make a homonym with the word for "together" or "concord," and the image of the twin boys thus became a symbol of concord and harmony between married couples. They also represent wealth, typically indicated by their precious and propitious emblems such as rhinoceros horn and coral, coins and ingots, and so on. In the present bottle, however, instead of a lotus the standing boy holds a toad, an emblem especially associated with another deity, Liu Hai (see cat. no. 16c).

The misuse or careless use of emblems is also found on the other side of the bottle. A bearded man on a raft is generally interpreted to be Zhang Qian, an official of the Western Han period (206 B.C.–A.D. 24). Zhang was twice dispatched as an envoy to the Western Regions (Xiyu, in today's Xinjiang and parts of Central Asia) in the late second century B.C., and these great journeys resulted in many interesting legends about him. One story tells that he was once sent to find the source of a river.[1] Reaching his goal after innumerable hardships, he drifted back on the current by raft. During his exploration he encountered the Weaving Maiden (Zhinü, living in the star Vega), who gave him a loom-supporting stone *(zhiji shi)*. Here a girl holding a long pole stands behind Zhang Qian and navigates the river, but with no stone in sight. A pomegranate hung from the raft symbolizes fertility, as it is full of seeds *(zi)*, or, more closely, full of male children, as the Chinese word *zi* can mean both seed and son. It is odd and rare, however, for a pomegranate to be depicted growing or hanging on Zhang Qian's raft. The only relevant explanation may be that he was believed to have brought the pomegranate tree to China from the Near East.

Notes
1. See Jin Guliang, *Manual of the Peerless* (Wushuang Pu), no. 5, the Wendetang edition. The book, published in 1690, lists forty famous people, including Zhang Qian, from the Han to the Song periods (206 B.C.–A.D. 1279), all considered unrivaled in their achievements. A portrait and a passage or poem are attached to each personage.

22 | TWO QUARTZ SNUFF
BOTTLES
18th–19th century
H. *(a)* 2⁵⁄₁₆ in. (5.8 cm),
(b) 1¾ in. (4.4 cm)
(a) 96.39.16, *(b)* 96.39.49

(a) The large bottle, agate of pale creamy tones with light yellow striated inclusions, flattened rounded rectangular shape on a flat oval base, carved around the neck with intaglio lines on both sides, incised on both shoulders with four characters wanshouwujiang *(everlasting longevity) and* bohetaihe *in seal script, very well hollowed, tourmaline stopper with ribbed lines matching those on the body.*

(b) The small bottle, quartz of dark reddish brown, of flattened circular shape resting on a slightly indented base, well hollowed, still with snuff inside, jadeite stopper with silver collar.

QUARTZ, AS A GENERIC TERM, covers a large variety of materials from which snuff bottles are made, including minerals within the quartz family whose composition cannot be readily classified. Such is the case of the small reddish brown bottle shown here.

These two bottles are noteworthy for their quiet, elegant forms and the innate beauty of the stones. The smaller bottle has no surface decoration, while the larger one is decorated merely with a few deceptively natural vertical lines. The shoulders of the larger bottle are inscribed with four characters reading "everlasting longevity," and, in seal script, *bohetaihe,* a philosophical term describing the opposing yet complementary state of *yin* and *yang,* the two most basic forces in nature. Bottles of this kind were suitable gifts for elders.

ROCK CRYSTAL IS THE PURE FORM of crystalline quartz. It is harder than nephrite (7 degrees on the Mohs scale). Prized as a metaphor for purity, this extremely durable stone was greatly cherished in China during the eighteenth and nineteenth centuries. Probably because of the symbolic meaning of rock crystal and the difficulty of carving it, bottles made from it by and large have simple, elegant forms with little or no surface decoration. This example, however, is from a small group of heavily decorated rock crystal bottles.[1]

Bottles carved with Spanish coin designs came into vogue during the first half of the nineteenth century.[2] The Spanish silver dollar, or eight reales, was minted during the reign of Charles IV (1788–1808) for the Spanish-American territories. In trade between China and the West, the currency became popular in Chinese seaports as its denomination and weight had the same value. Its use as a decorative motif on snuff bottles was clearly inspired by its exotic nature, a notion similar to the appearance of European paintings on enameled Chinese porcelain in the late eighteenth century.

The carving of this bottle is very skillful. The profile of the Spanish king was outlined accurately, and details such as facial muscles, arc lines for the thick hair, and wavy lines for the soft texture of the garment were all painstakingly supplied. In doing so, the carver successfully created a realistic, three-dimensional profile very different from a conventional Chinese portrait.

Notes
1. For related bottles, see Stevens, *The Collector's Book of Snuff Bottles,* no. 459, and Sin et al., eds., *A Congregation of Snuff Bottle Connoisseurs,* no. 215.
2. Sin et al., eds., *A Congregation of Snuff Bottle Connoisseurs,* no. 215.

23 | ROCK CRYSTAL SNUFF
BOTTLE
19th century
H. 1⅞ in. (4.7 cm)
96.39.41

Of flattened round shape, carved in relief on both sides with design of a Spanish silver dollar, on the front a profile of the Spanish king encircled with the clockwise inscription DEI. GRATIA. 1796. CAROLUS. IIII, *on the reverse a coat of arms encircled with the clockwise inscription* HISPAN. ETIND. REX. M. 8R. F. M., *well hollowed, grayish blue quartz stopper with tiger's-eye collar.*

INKSTONE, WHOSE NAME COMES FROM ITS WIDESPREAD USE as the material on which to grind ink, is a type of sedimentary rock. Although the Chinese tried varied materials, including ceramic, as a grinding surface, four preferred types emerged from about the tenth century.[1] Sedimentary rocks chosen for making inkstones *(yan* or *yantai)* are all very dense in texture and thus particularly suitable for grinding ink. The natural inclusions and color tones of the rocks are also appreciated. Well-designed and carved inkstones are highly valued artworks.

Inkstone was probably first employed as a material for snuff bottles during the late eighteenth century. Treated as a semiprecious stone, it was worked by the same lapidary means. The stone of the present bottle is fine grained with a purplish, dark brown color, typical of a type of rock quarried from the riverbanks at Duanxi in northern Guangdong province.[2] Regarded as the best for inkstones, the so-called *duan* stones have long been treasured in China. The carving of two *kui* dragons on the front is reminiscent of the low-relief carving often seen on inkstone decoration, and the four raised characters within a circle are clearly in imitation of a round seal imprint. In carrying such motifs, the bottle imparts a scholarly taste that is usually associated with inkstones and other accoutrements of the scholar's studio.

The *kui* dragon is a veteran motif of Chinese decorative arts. It characteristically has only one leg and is praised as the master of all dragons. Selective in diet, the *kui* dragon drinks only from clear springs and never touches turbid earth. It is therefore regarded as a symbol of purity and high morality, values that were prized by scholars.

Notes
1. The *duan* stone from the south (Guangdong province) is usually of warm tones with rich variations in grain and inclusion; the *she* stone, from the east (Zhejiang province) is of dusk tones; from the northwest come the yellowish green *taohe* stone (Gansu province) and the exceptional *chengni* inkstone (Shanxi province) of extremely fine-grained clay.

2. For a related bottle, see Kleiner, *Chinese Snuff Bottles,* pl. 16, right; for bottles made of other inkstones, see Stevens, *The Collector's Book of Snuff Bottles,* nos. 645, 647, and 660.

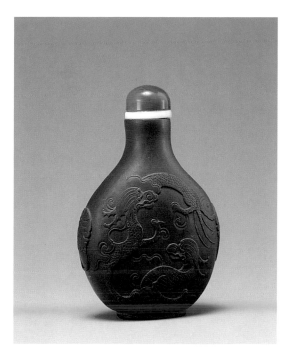

Of pear shape on a raised ring foot, carved in relief on the dark purplish brown stone with two kui dragons amid clouds on one side and four characters Duanxi zhenwan *(elegant plaything from Duanxi) in seal script on the other, adorned on each shoulder with a mock mask suspending a loop ring handle, agate stopper with an ivory collar.*

25 | PUDDINGSTONE SNUFF
BOTTLE
Late 18th–early 19th
century
H. 2⅛ in. (5.4 cm)
96.39.19

*Of round shape resting on a ring foot, with a short straight neck, the
buff matrix holding pebbles and chips of brown, gray, and russet colors,
well hollowed, coral stopper with green glass collar.*

AMONG THE SEMIPRECIOUS STONES, the most visually attractive is the so-
called puddingstone. A conglomerate of sedimentary rocks, puddingstone is
composed of a siliceous matrix that contains pebbles or fragments of flint and
quartz varying in size, shape, color, texture, and hardness. It was used to make
snuff bottles no later than the eighteenth century, as porcelain copies were
being made during that period.[1] But production was limited, perhaps because
the pebbles could easily fall out or the matrix crack during cutting and polishing, resulting in a high rate of failure.[2]

Although occasionally bearing simple geometrical panels and facets as
decoration, puddingstone bottles are usually plain, as in the present example,
for the natural pattern of the stone asserts a strong visual appeal that affords
both artistic spontaneity and uniqueness. Knowing that no two puddingstone
bottles are ever alike undoubtedly adds much to our delight in them.

Notes
1. Kleiner, *Chinese Snuff Bottles*, p. 48.
2. Hui and Sin, *An Imperial Qing Tradition*, p. 97.

Of cloudy, clear reddish yellow and black colors, carved in the form of a pebble with designs on both sides, on the front, the vertical black color reserved for a centipede with its antenna stretched out as if to hook a nearby indistinguishable object, on the reverse a rock garden setting, stem-shaped glass stopper of coral color with a silver collar.

AMBER, A PRECIOUS GEM OF ORGANIC ORIGIN, is the fossilized resin exuded millions of years ago from pines of a particular species now extinct. Light and warm to the touch, amber is reddish yellow in hue but shades from clear to black, and hence has various names. The best known are "golden amber," for transparent light yellow; "cherry amber," for reddish brown; "beeswax" or "Baltic amber," for opaque yellow; and "root amber," for cloudy, opaque, and uneven colors. Throughout the snuff bottle period, translucent brown amber from Burma (Myanmar) and opaque golden amber from the Baltic area of Russia were both available to the Chinese. Amber bottles were cherished at the court;[1] however, only a small number were made in the Qianlong reign (1736–95) and most existing amber bottles were products of the nineteenth century. Toward the late nineteenth century, amber snuff bottles were shipped to Japan for further embellishment with designs in lacquer and hardstones. Amber bottles were cut and polished by the same lapidary method as for stone but demanded more attention and care as amber is quite brittle and easily scratched.

On this bottle, a large area of the vertical black inclusions has been cleverly transformed into a centipede, its prominent size due to the deliberate adherence to the material's natural form and color. The carving is skillful. Lines and forms are confidently executed, and details like the body segments and numerous legs as well as the soft texture of the centipede are convincingly depicted. The motivation for such a design is not clear, as the poisonous centipede usually does not appear in Chinese artworks.[2] It is likely that the natural phenomenon of insects trapped in amber inspired the design, as well as the desire to cater to the natural form of the black inclusions. The present bottle appears to be unique as no other similar example has yet been recorded.

Notes
1. The collection of the National Palace Museum, Taipei, originally the imperial collection, includes some amber bottles. See Zhang, ed., *Snuff Bottles in the Collection of the National Palace Museum,* nos. 373–93.

2. Being one of the "five noxious creatures," the centipede is often grouped with the snake, the scorpion, the gecko, and the toad. A picture of Zhong Kui, a legendary demon queller, showing him busy slaying the five noxious creatures is a special talisman used on the fifth day of the fifth Chinese month for expelling these evils.

*Of flattened ovoid shape resting on an oval ring foot, carved through
the lime green overlay to the bubble-suffused translucent ground with
an all-around design of four connecting* chi *dragons, one of them holding a* lingzhi *fungus in its mouth, black speckles of trapped carbon in
the overlay glass, tourmaline stopper with a black vinyl collar.*

LIKE CERAMICS, GLASS IS A MAN-MADE MATERIAL. Since the fifth century
B.C. the Chinese manufactured glasswares from lead and barium, the distin-
guishing ingredients of all native Chinese glass. But because such glass is brittle
and easily broken, it never reached prominence in Chinese decorative arts.
Western glass, composed of soda and lime, had long been imported to China,
but its formula was unknown to the Chinese until the seventeenth century,
when Jesuits introduced it. Glass then became a major focus of the decorative
arts. Many exquisite artworks were created in the form of miniature snuff
bottles.

    According to several textual sources of the Qing dynasty (1644–1911), early
snuff bottles were made of glass.[1] The first known reference to the subject was
written by Wang Shizhen in 1703–4: "Recently snuff has also been made in the
capital. . . . It is stored in glass bottles. These glass bottles are of all shapes and
colors. While the white is like crystal and the red like fire, there are also purple,

yellow, black, and green and so on. These bottles are extremely adorable. . . . They are all made in the Palace [in the imperial glass factory]. Imitations are made elsewhere but never could they be comparable to the originals."[2] The imperial glass factory was established in 1696 under the direction of Killian Stumpff, a German Jesuit. Artisans mainly came from Guangzhou, in the south, and Boshan (called Yanshenzhen in the Qing dynasty), in the northeastern province of Shandong. They were able to produce monochrome glass of all colors, splashed gold glass *(sajinxing),* multicolored glass, and ground glass *(mohua);* they also invented overlay glass. In the eighteenth century, the golden era of Chinese glassmaking, artisans made great achievements both in the variety of glass types and in the originality of decoration. Glass overlay in particular was an area that saw great invention.

The single overlay glass bottle is made by dipping the glass body into a molten glass of another color to form a layer or coat. When hardened, this coat is carved through to form a design set off by the revealed original surface of a contrasting color. Both the carved relief design and the revealed ground surface were then smoothed and polished, and it was the patience and carefulness that the artisan showed in refining the bottle which determined its quality. Appreciation of overlay glass bottles is founded on three criteria: the quality of the glass itself (sometimes special effects are intended, such as bubbles or crizzling within the glass which evoke images like snowflakes or fishnets), the design, and its carving. The present example represents a high degree of excellence in all these areas. The white translucent ground and lime-green clear overlay form a genial color scheme, fresh and soothing. Four *chi* dragons roll and wander freely over the surface, creating a sense of movement as well as forming a dazzling arabesque pattern. One of the *chi* dragons holds in its mouth a *lingzhi* fungus, a symbol of long life. The carving is crisp and detailed. Expressive lines emphasize both forceful movement and facial and body features, and careful polishing brings out a sleek sheen to the surface. In its beautiful quality this bottle compares favorably with those from the imperial workshop of the eighteenth century.

detail
cat. no. 27

Notes

1. In *Secret Notes of Pengshan* (Pengshan Miji), Gao Shiqi, the tutor of classic prose and poetry to Emperor Kangxi, recorded that in 1704 the emperor Kangxi bestowed upon him several glasswares, including two snuff bottles; see Xia, ed., *Masterpieces of Snuff Bottles in the Palace Museum,* p. 2. Writing in *Casual Questions of the Valiant Studio* (Yonglu Xianjie), the earliest monograph on snuff and snuff bottles (1868), the famous connoisseur Zhao Zhiqian stated that the first snuff bottles to be manufactured were of glass; see "Casual Questions of the Valiant Studio," in *Chinese Art Series* (Zhongguo Meishu Congshu), edited by Deng Shi, vol. 2, pp. 201, 214, reprinted by International Culture Publishing (Guoji Wenhua Chuban Gongsi), 1993.

2. Wang Shizhen was minister of the Ministry of Justice during Emperor Kangxi's reign; see his book, *Notes of Orchid Studio* (Xiangzu Biji), vol. 7, p. 131, reprinted by Shanghai Ancient Books (Shanghai Guji Chubanshe), 1982.

WHILE THE TECHNIQUE OF GLASS OVERLAY was known during the Kangxi reign (1662–1722), records of the imperial workshop show that its production was limited to the Yongzhen and Qianlong reigns (1723–95), and its output was quite small in comparison with other glass snuff bottles. Not counting those bottles executed voluntarily by artisans, fewer than ten imperial orders were given for overlay glass snuff bottles over about seventy years.

Unlike the limited manufacture in the imperial glass factory, however, overlay snuff bottles were produced in large quantities at Yanshenzhen (now Boshan) in Shandong province and in Beijing over a long period. These commercial bottles have a large variety of shapes and a wide repertoire in overlay colors and decorative designs. They tend to vary greatly in quality, but there is no lack of superb examples, of which many were sent to the court as gifts or tributes. Most imperial overlay glass bottles are small in size and full bodied in form. Among them, single overlay bottles are typically red or blue on white and exquisite in design and carving. Some bear carved reign marks at their bases. Outside the palace the imperial bottles were eagerly imitated in wares such as the present example. Not only the *chi* dragon motif but its apparent elegance and delicacy are reminiscent of imperial taste. Both the ground and overlay glasses are pure and clear, with a pleasing contrast between the milky white and azure blue. When the opalescent white body is suffused with light, the refinement of the design is further enhanced as the blue *chi* dragon seems to swim in the void.

28 | SINGLE OVERLAY GLASS
SNUFF BOTTLE
Early 19th century
H. 2¾ in. (7 cm)
96.39.21

Of elongated pear shape resting on a round ring foot, carved through the blue overlay to the opalescent white ground with a writhing chi *dragon on both sides, jadeite stopper with a black vinyl collar.*

ABOUNDING WITH RAW MATERIALS, the town of Yanshenzhen (now Boshan), in Shandong province, was an important supplier of glass. The glass lumps or rods manufactured there, in various colors, were sent to workshops in Beijing to be melted again and molded or blown, or to be carved directly in the lapidary method. The lapidary workers regarded glass as a kind of stone, and they shaped it by cutting or grinding, just as they did stone. As a result, glass was valued on a level equivalent to semiprecious stone, and it remained expensive until the late nineteenth century.[1]

Glass snuff bottles were produced in the imperial glass factory no later than the beginning of the eighteenth century. They were favored by the emperor and his courtiers both for personal use and as gifts to others.[2] Compared with other products of the imperial workshops, glass snuff bottles enjoyed a long production life which was marked by their rich variety, including monochrome glass, overlay glass, mottled glass *(jiao boli)* with streaks or spots in varied tints or colors, gold-star glass *(jinxing boli)* with gorgeous tiny gold speckles formed in firing and then carved in the lapidary method, and gold-flecked glass *(sajinxing boli)* with splashed gold drops. Besides the imperial workshop, commercial workshops also produced all these types of glass bottles, and continued to do so into the early twentieth century. The large proportion of glass bottles among the snuff bottles presented to the court by local officials as gifts or tributes testifies to their vast output.

The *chi* dragon was a popular motif of the period. On this bottle, three *chi* dragons in white overlay sprawl conspicuously across a blue background. The design tries to stimulate new interest by reversing the conventional dark-on-light decorative scheme.

Notes
1. Stevens, *The Collector's Book of Snuff Bottles,* p. 78.

2. In 1755 Emperor Qianlong ordered on the seventh day of the fourth month that five hundred glass snuff bottles and three thousand glasswares be made for presentation to those who played essential roles in military conquest of the northwestern region of the empire; see Yang Boda, "The Palace Workshops and Imperial Kilns Snuff Bottles of Emperor Qianlong," *Arts of Asia* 26, no. 5 (September–October 1996): 70.

29 | SINGLE OVERLAY GLASS
SNUFF BOTTLE
19th century
H. 2¾ in. (7 cm)
96.39.24

Of elongated, olive shape with a straight neck and a flaring ring foot, carved through the white overlay to the opaque turquoise-blue ground with three chi dragons twining around the bottle, tourmaline stopper with yellow glass collar.

SYMBOLIC MOTIFS HAVE LONG DOMINATED designs of Chinese art. Their function is secular rather than religious, and they are generally concerned with the basic themes of a long and healthy life, high civic and social rank, and abundant male offspring. Because one has to ponder the image for clues to its meaning, the Chinese find pictorial metaphors far more subtle and interesting than words for expressing these worldly wishes. Chinese decorative arts are therefore replete with symbolic motifs that delight both the eye and the ear.

The symbols on this bottle form two rebuses, but they can also be read with several other meanings depending on whether they are viewed as single motifs or grouped motifs. Above all, the shared meaning is love. Fish and water are a metaphor for sexual intercourse; a happily married couple may be described as having "the pleasures like fish in water" *(ruyu deshui)*. Here a pair of goldfish swimming in a pond represents harmony and sexual pleasure. On the reverse is a scene of a lotus pond. Chinese words for lotus, pronounced *lian* or *he,* are phonetically identical with the words for binding, connection *(lian),* or concord, unison *(he)*. A picture of a lotus leaf and blossom on one stem therefore expresses the wish for "shared heart and harmony." When the lotus leaf and blossom are grouped with a lotus seedpod, a symbol of fertility, they form another rebus, meaning "may you continually have sons" *(liansheng guizi)*. Brimming with these meanings of love, the bottle is an ideal gift for a wedding.

Overlay glass in orange-brown is unusual, and the naturalistic touches in the generally static design on this bottle are noteworthy. Lively incised lines describe bird feathers, plant veins, and waves; embossed dots stand for lotus seeds. The curling edges of the lotus are expressively rendered in thick overlay glass, but the waves appear static and the fish and pond are ill-proportioned. Clearly the motifs serve more as carriers of symbolic meaning than elements for realistic representation.

30 | SINGLE OVERLAY GLASS
SNUFF BOTTLE
Late 18th–early 19th century
H. 2¹³⁄₁₆ in. (7.2 cm)
96.39.26

Of ovoid shape, clear body with tiny snowflake inclusions, overlaid with a layer of orange-brown through which is carved an overall design of a lotus pond, on one side two goldfish swimming, on the reverse a lotus plant flanked by an arrowhead with a bird above in flight, coral-colored glass stopper with tiger's-eye collar.

THIS BOTTLE IS AN EXAMPLE OF THE SEAL SCHOOL, which prevailed during the first half of the nineteenth century. The name of the school seems to have derived from seal-script inscriptions that often accompany the designs. Glass bottles of the Seal School tend to have circular or ovoid forms, and generally have low relief carved through overlay to an opaque white ground. Its subjects are similar to those of contemporary Chinese paintings and in some cases resemble well-known paintings of the Eight Eccentrics of Yangzhou of the eighteenth century.[1]

Combining the bat and *shoudai* bird (phonetic symbols of good luck and longevity) with *lingzhi* fungus and *taihu* rocks (also symbols of longevity), the design produces pictorial rebuses as "best wishes for good fortune and for longevity." The two phoenixes among blossoms symbolize conjugal felicity.

The delicate taste of this bottle characterizes the style of the Seal School. Forms are cursive and full of vitality. Lines and shapes are simple yet expressive and convincing, whether depicting the rough texture of rock and bark or supple and tender blossoms. The spacious settings and the subdued color achieve a rare elegance and tranquillity.

The inscription "riding the wind, the most exquisite fragrance" is a poetic line, but the seal reading "black cloud" is likely a studio name. Judging by the motifs, style, and fine execution, this bottle may be tentatively attributed to Li Junting, the foremost artist of the Seal School.[2]

Notes

1. Clare Lawrence, "An Analysis of the Seal School Group of Glass Snuff Bottles," *Journal of the International Chinese Snuff Bottle Society* 25, no. 2 (Summer 1993): 9. The Eight Eccentrics were all literati, well versed in letters and poetry as well as calligraphy. They were not professional painters in the traditional sense, but they sold paintings for a living in Yangzhou. Pursuing personal styles quite removed from orthodox modes, they favored a direct presentation of ideas and feelings. Their favorite subjects were flowers, plants, and birds.

2. For Li's other bottles, see Sin et al., eds., *A Congregation of Snuff Bottle Connoisseurs,* nos. 70–71, and Lawrence, *Miniature Masterpieces,* no. 130. Bottles attributed to Li Junting are usually of the highest quality, bearing the best designs and a fine execution unparalleled in the school. The motifs of his bottles usually include *taihu* rocks and birds, flowers, and plants. Li's seal or sometimes his name appear on some of these bottles. A bottle in the collection of Mary and George Bloch is signed "Mr. Li of Jingjiang" with the seal "Junting" and a date corresponding to 1819 (Lawrence, "Analysis of the Seal School Group," p. 12).

31 | SINGLE OVERLAY GLASS
SNUFF BOTTLE
1800–1850
H. 2¼ in. (5.7 cm)
96.39.22

Of flattened circular shape, green overlay on an opaque milky white ground, on the front carved with a bat hovering above and a shoudai (paradise flycatcher) perching on bamboo by taihu (Lake Tai) rocks, a lingzhi *fungus at the left, a seal-script inscription reading* zhanfeng yipinxiang *(riding the wind, the most exquisite fragrance) at the right, the reverse of similar design but with two phoenixes, one in flight and the other perching on a blossoming plum tree, a seal reading* heiyun *(black cloud) to the left, animal masks with ring handles on the shoulders, pink glass stopper with green glass collar.*

32 | SINGLE OVERLAY GLASS
SNUFF BOTTLE
Early 19th century
H. 2⅜ in. (6 cm)
96.39.25

*Of circular shape, the opaque pink body overlaid in bluish green,
carved with an overall design of gourd vines, glass stopper and collar
of coral red and bluish green.*

AS SEEN IN PREVIOUS EXAMPLES, overlay bottles are typically created by dipping a bottle into molten glass of another color to form a uniform coat of one
even tone. The bluish green overlay on this bottle, however, seems to have been
added to the pink body in lines and blobs. Darker or lighter shades of color
seen in the vines and gourds of the design attest to this irregular application.
When added, the lines and blobs could be retouched to form desired shapes.
Such a technique offered a considerable savings in the time and labor required
to carve away the overlay to reveal the ground, and to polish both the overlay
and ground surfaces. The subject of gourds suspended on continuous vines
implies a wish for abundant offspring through generations (see cat. no. 4 for a
discussion of the symbolic meaning of gourds).

DOUBLE OVERLAY GLASS
SNUFF BOTTLE
1800–1860
H. 2⅝ in. (6.8 cm)
96.39.23

Of circular shape, carved through the double overlay of white and black to the translucent snowflake ground with an all-around design of a magpie perching on a gnarly blossoming plum tree (repeated on each side), coral-colored glass stopper with a half-bead pearl finial and black vinyl collar.

INNOVATION ON THE SINGLE OVERLAY TECHNIQUE resulted in double or triple overlay, in which bottles were dipped into two or three different colors. This led to even more elaborate multicolor overlay, whereby up to eight colors were applied not in layers but in patches to different parts of the body so that one overlay of multiple hues was achieved.

The present bottle was coated successively with black and white overlays, and then carved through to the original ground.[1] The white overlay on top is reserved in the form of plum blossoms and snow on the tree, while the black overlay is carved to form the trunk and branches. Air bubbles trapped in the glass bring forth the snowflake appearance of the ground. It provides a perfect setting for the theme of the wintry plum, which stresses the tree's lofty and unyielding character as its blossoms defiantly brave frost and snow. The design includes a magpie, repeated at the left edge on each side, perching on the tip of a plum branch and holding a tiny sprig in its mouth. To the Chinese, the

magpie is a bird that brings joy. Together with the place where it perches and the action it performs, the magpie forms two rebuses, "happiness is just coming" *(xishan meishao)* and "chirping magpie heralds the arrival of the spring" *(xibao chunxian)*. The symbolism imbedded in the overall design pronounces two cherished qualities: firm and steadfast against harsh environments, and positive and optimistic about the future.

Notes
1. There is another fine bottle in the Seattle Art Museum's collection with a similar style but different design, of a deer in a wintry landscape; see Stevens, *The Collector's Book of Snuff Bottles,* no. 227.

Rock crystal, of flattened rounded rectangular shape resting on a ring foot, painted in colors with a continuous garden scene with insects among rock work and plants, on one side a cricket on a branch among flowers and a dragonfly in flight, on the reverse a butterfly and a dragonfly over a row of rocks by chrysanthemum blossoms, an inscription and signature in running script reading "made by Zhou Leyuan after the style of Xinluo shanren in the hot summer of 1887," followed by a red square seal reading yin *(seal), coral-colored glass stopper with black vinyl collar.*

INTERIOR OR "INSIDE" PAINTING is the most recently developed technique for the decoration of snuff bottles, although scholars still dispute when the style might have originated.[1] A bottle dated 1815 and signed Gan Xuan, however, is by and large accepted as the earliest dated inside-painted bottle in existence,[2] and Gan Xuan as the earliest artist so far known to have worked in the medium.[3]

Inside-painted snuff bottles are usually of rock crystal or glass, media whose transparent surfaces allow easy viewing of the painting. To ensure adherence of the water-based paints, the smooth interior surface is roughened, achieving a frosted effect whose whiteness also acts as a background to the design. Spending a month or more to finish one bottle, painters used special pens made of bamboo slivers or fine brushes, with the tip bent at a right angle to touch the inside surface.

detail
cat. no. 34

Regarded as the founder of the Beijing School (c. 1881–present), the artist Zhou Leyuan most actively worked in the capital city from 1881 to 1893. Specializing in landscapes, he also excelled in subjects such as insects and plants. His works were very much admired and copied by his contemporaries and later artists.

The inscription on the bottle indicates that the painting is in the manner of Xinluo shanren, an important innovative master of bird-and-flower painting active in the middle of the Qing dynasty.[4] Xinluo shanren's distinctive style is manifested in a dexterous yet subtle brushwork as well as in beautiful, tasteful coloring. His ability to animate the liveliest moments of his subjects makes his paintings expressive and spirited, and a great feast to the eye.

The diagonal composition of the cricket and rock work, Zhou Leyuan's favorite motifs, was obviously inspired by Xinluo shanren, but Zhou's dramatization of it makes it his own. His brushwork is virtuoso. Dots, lines, and washes are confidently and skillfully applied to appropriate forms and textures. Details like the insects' wings are all meticulously depicted whether mottled or transparent, as are the various plant leaves. Chrysanthemums are in full bloom, while grass grows vigorously over the craggy rocks. Like his great model, Zhou was adept at catching the instantaneousness of a moment, as vividly depicted here in the different movements of the insects.

Reflecting his deep admiration for the master, Zhou left a group of bottles painted and inscribed in the manner of Xinluo shanren. In doing so, Zhou formed his own refined and lofty painting style, enabling him to stand out as one of the greatest artists in the genre of inside painted bottles.

Notes
1. One view holds that the technique was first practiced during the late Qianlong reign of the late eighteenth century, while the other favors the Guangxu reign of the late nineteenth century.

2. Now in the collection of the Art Museum, Princeton University (Y1936-590), this crystal bottle is an unusual elongated oval with slightly broader shoulders. It is painted within on both sides in elegant colors and fine brushstrokes. On one side is a towering pine tree with rock work and orchid at its root, two seven-character poetry lines, and a signature in the artist's fancy name, Gugang jushi; on the reverse is a beautiful landscape in the style of the Orthodox School of the Qing dynasty, topped with a poem, signed with the name of Gan Xuan, and dated to the fourth month of 1815. The interior is stained by snuff to light brown with some worn spots. I am indebted to Cary Liu, associate curator of Asian Art at Princeton's Art Museum, who kindly allowed me to study the bottle.

3. Gan Xuan is the same person as Gan Xuanwen. For discussion of this artist and his works, see Hugh Moss, "The Lingnan School of Snuff Bottle Interior Painters, Introduction and Part I: Gan Xuanwen," *Journal of the International Chinese Snuff Bottle Society* 23, no. 1 (Spring 1991): 4–20.

4. The artist's formal name is Hua Yan (1682–1756); Xinluo shanren is his fancy name. A native of Fujian province, Hua Yan settled at Yangzhou where he earned his living through painting.

LANDSCAPE WAS ONE OF ZHOU LEYUAN'S SPECIALTIES, and it perhaps affords the best display of his consummate painting skill. Masterfully using various brushstrokes to represent the different textures of rock, plant, and water, he controlled the crystal surface with as much confidence as he would paint on paper. The gentle slopes of the mountain range, of a typical southern type, are covered with moss and grass, with a chain of mounds reserved in blank or light color to represent the undulating hills. In the middle ground, a small boat indicates a water scene. On the grassy riverbank in the foreground are four sturdy willows with newly emerged leaves. Their twigs sway in the breeze, permeating the soft green scene with an air of spring.

The reverse scene is also rich in form and content, composed of motifs typical of the scholar's taste. The subject belongs to the "picture of antiquities" *(bogu tu)*, a classic theme echoing the typical ambience preferred by a Confucian scholar and emphasizing the importance of refined taste and connoisseurship. Besides being admired for their formal beauty, the potted pine and plum are symbols of the lofty and unyielding, and the jagged *taihu* rock connotes the firm and steadfast. Together they become a miniature of the natural world, the place to which the scholar longs to retreat and find nourishment. The dark incense burner at the far right is in the shape of a bronze tripod, and the crackles of the large vase suggest the distinctive glaze pattern of precious *guan* stoneware. These objects and miniatures are the very accoutrements that scholars would choose for their studios.

The artist did not date the bottle. But judging by its high quality and by comparison with a bottle by Zhou Leyuan of similar *bogu tu* design and style dated 1892,[1] this bottle is datable to about 1892, the very end of Zhou's late active period. He did not paint after 1893.

Notes
1. See Xia, ed., *Masterpieces of Snuff Bottles in the Palace Museum,* no. 210.

Rock crystal, of flattened rounded rectangular shape on a ring foot, painted on both sides with elegant colors, on one side a landscape with windblown trees at the foreground, a small boat in the middle ground and undulating mountains in the far distance, on the reverse side a still-life scene with a taihu rock, a vase of plum blossoms, an incense burner and a potted miniature pine, a dedicatory inscription in running script reading "made by Zhou Leyuan at Lushe in Xuannan, for the pure appreciation of the respected elder brother Guzeng," followed by a red seal (to be deciphered), turquoise stopper carved with a design of a coiling chi *dragon and silver collar.*

ALTHOUGH SIGNED WITH ZHOU LEYUAN'S NAME, the painting is a copy after the master's style. Instead of an organic representation of natural elements, the composition here is more a design of formalized patterns. Particularly stylized are the netlike mounds of the mountain range and the static patterns of the tree leaves.[1] It is no surprise that the tremendous influence and fame of Zhou Leyuan resulted in a great number of bottles painted after his style or even forged with his name. Whether for the purpose of admiration or commercial gain, these bottles for the most part are confined to his classical subjects such as landscape, seen here, insects and plants, and goldfish. Almost all his followers in the Beijing School produced similar works.

Zhou Leyuan was among the few artists practicing inside-painting who excelled in calligraphy. His fluent writing has a distinctively free style, as seen on the previous examples. The calligraphy of the two inscriptions here, however, was written stiffly with flat strokes and sharp angles, reminiscent of many works of the Ye family. It is thus this author's assumption that the bottle may have been painted by the Ye family. The light melancholy tone of the inscribed poem, also a copy of a Zhou original, echoes well the tranquil atmosphere of the landscape. It reads:

> Upright green hills reflect white clouds
> Under the setting sun are dogs and chickens and a small village
>   of several families,
> Empty river has no home-coming fishermen
> Peach blossoms have withered and it is time to close the door.[2]

Notes
1. For bottles similar in subject and composition but from Zhou's own hand, see Xia, ed., *Masterpieces of Snuff Bottles in the Palace Museum,* no. 211; Hui and Sin, *An Imperial Qing Tradition,* no. 208; and Little and Silver, *The World in a Bottle,* B11.

2. For the exact same poem on a genuine bottle by Zhou, see Susan Hacker and Y. F. Yung "Inside-painted Snuff Bottles," *Journal of the International Chinese Snuff Bottle Society* 15, no. 1 (Spring 1983): 9, fig. 1.

Rock crystal, of flattened rounded rectangular shape on a ring foot, painted in colors with a landscape continuing on both sides, in the foreground two scholars stroll toward a riverside cottage where a person reads inside with a fisherman poling a boat across the river in the middle ground with mountains in the far distance, a 28-character poem inscribed at the top of one side, together with the name of Zhou Leyuan and two red seals, one with the characters yuan yin *(seal of [Zhou Le]yuan) and the other to be deciphered, the top of the reverse side inscribed "made by Zhou Leyuan in the mid-autumn of 1892 at the Studio of the Fragrance of Lotus-root in Dumen [the capital, Beijing]," and followed by a red seal with the characters* yuan yin, *pink glass stopper with ocher glass collar.*

YAN YUTIAN WAS AMONG THE BEST FOLLOWERS of Zhou Leyuan. He started his career by imitating Zhou's works but later formed his own distinctive brushwork and a palette of light brown and ink black. His mature works include various subjects such as landscapes and pond scenes with insects and plants as well as animals like the buffalo and donkey. He liked to use ink wash directly to form motifs without outlines, which, together with an overall light tone, create an idyllic yet expressive effect.

The dates of Yan's birth and death are not certain. As to his active working period, one theory claims the interval from 1890 to 1907, and another from 1895 to 1918.[1] The present bottle was signed as being made by Leyuan but is also unmistakably affixed with a large red seal giving Yan's name, Yutian. The use of both the great master's name and the artist's own indicates clearly that this bottle was not a forgery intended to deceive but a copy of Zhou's original work, intended to express Yan's great admiration for Zhou Leyuan as well as pride at being his follower. The date 1888 is more likely that of the Zhou original than of the copy. Before 1895, in his early career, Yan mainly concentrated on learning from the master, as in the present example. From about 1895 onward, however, he started to produce mature works of his own.[2]

The subjects depicted here are clearly from Zhou Leyuan's repertoire, but the rendering is a little more restrained. The delicate tone and the reliance on light washes or shades forecast Yan Yutian's later stylistic characteristics.

The Chinese word "goldfish" *(jinyu)* is phonetically identical with another two words meaning "gold in abundance" or "gold and jade" *(jin yu)*. The motif of goldfish thus expresses a wish for abundant wealth. A boy riding a water buffalo and flying a kite is another auspicious motif, meant to express wishes for soaring aspirations and high spirits.

Notes
1. See Little and Silver, *The World in a Bottle,* p. 88, and Hui and Sin, *An Imperial Qing Tradition,* p. 180.

2. For Yan Yutian's mature works, see Hui and Sin, *An Imperial Qing Tradition,* no. 215; Lawrence, *Miniature Masterpieces,* no. 144; and Little and Silver, *The World in a Bottle,* no. B12.

37 | INSIDE-PAINTED SNUFF
BOTTLE
c. 1895
By Yan Yutian
H. 2⅛ in. (5.4 cm)
96.39.34

Rock crystal, of flattened rounded rectangular shape on a thin ring foot, painted in elegant colors on one side with two pictures in the form of album leaves, one fan-shaped with two goldfish and the other rectangular with a boy flying a kite on the back of a water buffalo, on the reverse side a painting of various antiquities (bogu tu), *an elongated square vase at the center surrounded clockwise by a squat pot of peony blossoms, ancient bronze coins, a* taihu *rock, and an incense burner, at the top an inscription reading "made by Leyuan in 1888," but a red seal revealing the name of the actual artist, Yutian, glass stopper of coral color with a tiny finial of white glass bead.*

38 INSIDE-PAINTED SNUFF
BOTTLE
Winter 1895
By Ding Erzhong
H. 2⅜ in. (6 cm)
96.39.36

Rock crystal of flattened rounded rectangular shape on a ring foot, painted in colors on one side with a wintry landscape in which a man on a donkey crosses a bridge and turns his head toward a blossoming plum tree at the right, mountains with a waterfall lying in the far distance, a couplet inscribed at the upper left reading "crossing a little bridge by donkey, sighing alone about those thin plum blossoms," signed Ding Erzhong with a red seal with the character ding, *on the reverse a scene of insects and plants on a grassy bank, some reeds at the back and a large* baisong *(Chinese cabbage) in front, and two goldfish beneath an aged overhanging branch, a dedicatory inscription and signature reading "made by Erzhong after the style of Weng Xiaohai in the winter of 1895 in Xuannan, for the respected inspector, the elder brother Zigui," followed by a red seal with the character* zhong, *pink glass stopper with a walrus ivory collar.*

DING ERZHONG WAS REGARDED AS THE MOST ACCOMPLISHED painter in the medium of inside-painting. Although literature on his life and career is elusive, he is generally believed to have been a seal carver, a painter, and a scholar, and he is one of the few snuff bottle artists to be listed in *The Dictionary of Chinese Artists' Names.*[1] In contrast to his fellow snuff bottle painters, he did not paint for commercial gain but for his own enjoyment or to create presentation pieces for friends. Consequently his works are rare, and very few bottles painted by him are in existence. His works are excellent in their literati taste and superb execution. Subject matter is scarcely repeated. He liked to follow the styles of various masters of Chinese painting, and in each of his works he demonstrated his complete understanding of the essence of different painting styles as well as his own consummate brushwork. His active working period is generally thought to have lasted from 1895 to 1905.

The sparse, wintry landscape on this bottle is reminiscent of paintings of the Wu School. Based on the scenery in Suzhou (then called Wu), in Jiangsu province, it was the leading school of literati painting in the fifteenth and sixteenth centuries, producing such illustrious artists as Shen Zhou and Wen Zhengming. Carrying on the traditions of the Northern Song masters and the brushwork of the Four Great Masters of the late Yuan period, the Wu School painters emphasized the importance of literary cultivation and the interplay between literary and visual expression. The influence of the Wu School was so profound that its style continued to be practiced in the nineteenth century. Being a native of Nantong in the area of Wu, Ding Erzhong would have readily encountered and learned from many masterful paintings of the Wu School.

The wintry landscape on the bottle imparts a lofty, elegant air. A broad stream formed by the sheer waterfall runs diagonally from the upper right to lower left, separating the foreground from the distant mountains. While the overall composition is simple and slender, individual elements are richly depicted with consummate brushwork. There are long hemp strokes for the texture of mountain rock, simple lines for the flowing water, little thin lines for the pine needles but stubby ones for the plum branches, and dots for the moss on the mounds and for the sparse plum blossoms. All are superbly executed with confidence and precision. They not only form a three-dimensional landscape but also produce a richly decorated surface. The light color tones and ink washes give a tranquil quality to the painting. The inscribed couplet, employing such words as "little," "alone," and "thin," echoes the austerity of the wintry scenery.

Notes
1. He was, however, merely recorded as a seal carver by his formal name, Ding Shangyu; see Yu Jianhua, ed., *The Dictionary of Chinese Artists' Names* (Zhongguo Meishujia Renming Cidian) (Shanghai: Shanghai's People's Press of Fine Arts, 1989), p. 4.

MA SHAOXUAN, A NATIVE OF BEIJING, was born in 1867 and died in 1939.[1] He was reportedly a follower of Zhou Leyuan and active from 1894 to 1925. He excelled in an enormous variety of subjects but was most famous for his portraits and calligraphy.[2] His bottles are often composed of a painting on one side and calligraphy on the other.

The crane and pine tree, a time-honored subject in Chinese decorative arts, symbolize wishes for longevity *(songhe changchun)*. Combined with peonies, an emblem of wealth and distinction, they also form a rebus meaning "riches, reputation, and long life" *(fugui changchun)*. The painting on this example is not executed with Ma's usual superbness, and is probably from the hand of a pupil. Nonetheless, it was done with meticulous effort and realistically depicts the varied natural forms such as pine bark, pine branches, and herbaceous peony leaves.

The reverse is inscribed with a paragraph quoted from a famous essay, "Preface to the Gathering at Lanting," composed in 353 by Wang Xizhi, the most famous Chinese calligrapher. It reads:

> On this day, the sky is clear and bright, the breeze gentle and pleasant
> Looking up to admire the infinity of the cosmos, looking down to see
>   the abundance of things
> Let your eyes travel at ease, and release the rein of your thoughts and
>   feelings so you can see and hear the utmost
> It truly is a pleasure.

Calligraphy is particularly difficult to render in this medium, for it demands clear presentation in a miniature size with little room for retouching. The lines here are well balanced and characters elegantly written, demonstrating an excellent mastery of the art form. Ma's calligraphy seems well suited for the peaceful mood conveyed by the essay.

Notes

1. Xia, ed., *Masterpieces of Snuff Bottles in the Palace Museum,* p. 12.

2. For Ma Shaoxuan's wide-ranging works, see Stevens, *The Collector's Book of Snuff Bottles,* nos. 832–52, 855–64, and Sin et al., eds., *A Congregation of Snuff Bottle Connoisseurs,* nos. 291–98.

39 | INSIDE-PAINTED SNUFF
BOTTLE
Midsummer 1900
By Ma Shaoxuan
H. 2¼ in. (5.7 cm)
96.39.40

Rock crystal, of flattened rounded rectangular shape on a ring foot, painted in colors on one side with a crane standing under a pine tree and blossoming peonies nearby, on the reverse an inscription in regular script of forty characters in black, dated midsummer 1900 and signed Ma Shaoxuan, followed by a red seal with the characters shaoxuan, *coral-colored glass stopper with an ivory collar.*

AN INSCRIPTION ABOVE THE LANDSCAPE PAINTING on this bottle refers to the so-called Four Great Masters of the late Yuan period: Huang Gongwang (1269–1355), Wu Zhen (1280–1354), Ni Zan (1301–74), and Wang Meng (1301–85). The "three-distance" composition, in which faraway mountains are separated by water in the middle ground from mounds with trees in the foreground, is reminiscent of Ni Zan's style but more complex. The long hemp strokes of the high mountains imitate the brush method of Huang Gongwang. The warm tone of the painting, however, produced by light colors and washes, is actually more in keeping with the style of the Wu School of the Ming dynasty, a stylistic descendant of the four Yuan masters.

In the usual manner for such bottles, the reverse is decorated with calligraphy, an essay of forty-eight characters that transcribes the famous "Commemoration of a Humble Room" (Loushi Ming), written by Liu Yuxi (772–842) of the Tang dynasty. It reads:

> Mountain is spirited by immortals rather than height
> Water is inspired by dragons rather than depth
> This is a humble room but filled with fragrance of virtues
> Green moss traces the steps, and green grass casts shades inside the
>   bamboo curtain
> Talking and laughing are all erudites, coming and going there are
>   no ignoramuses.

Some elements of the painting seem to correspond with the inscription, yet it is impossible to know whether the painting was directly inspired by the prose or just elegant company. The calligraphy once again proves Ma Shaoxuan's matchless virtuosity in this unique domain. Demonstrating his seasoned confidence and skill, Ma neatly formed the overall structure in perfect balance, despite the bottle's narrow panel and the length of the prose. Each stroke is conscientiously written, and each character masterfully constructed in a uniform size.

The quadrangular bottle was made by blowing glass into a mold. All the sharp edges of the outer shape were flattened to make more facets to better reflect light, probably in imitation of rock crystal. The different profiles of the exterior and interior walls create the impression of a bottle within a bottle and show the painting to better effect.

40 | INSIDE-PAINTED
SNUFF BOTTLE
Fifth month, 1903
By Ma Shaoxuan
H. 2⁵⁄₁₆ in. (5.8 cm)
96.39.28

Glass, of flattened quadrangular shape with rounded shoulders and a rectangular ring foot, painted in colors on four sides, on the front a landscape painting together with an inscription "made in the capital after the style of the Yuan masters" and a red seal with the character ma, *on the reverse an inscription in regular script of an essay, on one narrow side signed Ma Shaoxuan and two red square seals with the characters* shao *and* xuan, *and on the other a date to the summer of the fifth month of 1903, dark green glass stopper with black vinyl collar.*

IT IS BELIEVED THAT MA SHAOXIAN was a nephew and a pupil of Ma Shaoxuan, and that he painted from 1899 to 1939. The relationship between the two artists thus destined their similar styles and subject matter. Close examination of Ma Shaoxian's work reveals that, except for the few finest examples of his late period, his paintings and calligraphy are not up to the high standard of his great mentor, and overall they tend to be uneven in quality. Despite his forty-year career, there are not as many bottles bearing his signature as his uncle's. It is likely that he more often signed his uncle's name than his own.

The subject of the lotus pond is again one of Zhou Leyuan's classic motifs, testifying to their continued popularity among followers of the Beijing School. The style of the painting echoes that of Zhou Leyuan's great model, Hua Yan's depiction of a lotus flower.[1] Through copy after copy, however, it lost its pure, elegant charm and, here, in the hands of Ma Shaoxian became formalized and static.

The poem on the reverse is inscribed in the style of Ma Shaoxuan. Though each character is clearly written, the strokes are less sturdy and forceful, the structure is not so well proportioned, and the spaces between the characters are not evenly balanced. When compared to his mentor's or his own later works, this bottle appears obviously to be from Ma Shaoxian's apprentice period.

It is not clear whether the poem was composed by the artist or someone else. An ode to the four seasons, it reads:

> Peach blossoms shine in red along the riverbank in spring
> Lotus leaves fill the pond in summer
> Osmanthus fragrance is wafted by breezes in autumn
> Snow witnesses the company of cold plum and old pine in winter.

As the present bottle presents only a summer view, it is likely that the bottle was originally one of a set of four.

Notes
1. The painting *Lotus Flower* by Hua Yan is now in the collection of the Palace Museum, Beijing; see Gao Meiqing, ed., *Paintings by Yangzhou Artists of the Qing Dynasty from the Palace Museum* (Gugong Bowuyuan Cang Qingdai Yangzhou Huajia Zuopin) (Hong Kong: The Palace Museum and the Art Gallery, the Chinese University of Hong Kong: 1984), p. 140, no. 36.

41 | INSIDE-PAINTED SNUFF
BOTTLE
Mid-spring 1914
By Ma Shaoxian
H. 2³⁄₁₆ in. (5.5 cm)
96.39.38

Glass, of flattened rounded rectangular shape on an oval ring foot, painted in light colors on one side with a blossoming lotus pond in which a school of fish swims, a dragonfly above in flight and a title inscription reading lianke jidi *(continuously passing the imperial examinations), the other side with a poem of twenty-eight characters in regular script in black, dated mid-spring 1914 and signed "made in Xuannan, Ma Shaoxian" with a red square seal with the character* shao, *pale green jade stopper.*

YE ZHONGSAN, A NATIVE OF BEIJING, was born in 1875 and died in 1945. Like Ma Shaoxuan, he was a versatile follower of Zhou Leyuan whose talents extended to just about every subject. He started painting in 1892 in Zhou's style and on many fine pieces he even signed Zhou's name. From 1895, however, he gradually developed his own style and was particularly renowned for his figure paintings, which are mostly narrative scenes from well-known novels and folklore.

The subject and the overall composition of this painting are reminiscent of those of Zhou Leyuan; however, forms like the pine tree and the heavy color tones are clearly of Ye Zhongsan's own style. As he did in other bottles, Ye centered the huge trunk of the pine tree on one side of the bottle, from where it branches in two and then into many small horizontal limbs that cross over the upper surface to the other side. He then added other motifs beneath the tree and at its crotch; mountains rise in the background. Once this formula was established, it became a standard Ye family tradition.[1]

The dumpy Mongolian horse and the monkey are Ye Zhongsan's favorite animal motifs. Their body structures are executed with fine anatomical detail, and they appear in vivid poses and gestures. The brushwork is confident, shifting freely between outlining and ink wash. While the pine and the *lingzhi* funguses symbolize longevity, the horse, monkey, and the bee, with calculated locations in the picture, form the rebus "may you be immediately conferred with the rank of marquis" *(mashang fenghou),* an auspicious wish for promotion to a higher office. A bottle decorated with these motifs was thus suitable for a respected uncle.

Notes
1. A later bottle painted by one of his sons is seen with the same composition of pine tree but different motifs of birds and flowers; see Hugh Moss, "The Apricot Grove Studio: The Works of the Ye Family, The Artists," *Journal of the International Chinese Snuff Bottle Society* 16, no. 1 (Spring 1984): 64, fig. 184.

42 | INSIDE-PAINTED SNUFF
BOTTLE
Autumn 1895
By Ye Zhongsan
H. 2⁷⁄₁₆ in. (6.7 cm)
96.39.29

Glass, of flattened rounded rectangular shape on a ring foot, painted in colors with a pine tree at the foreground with branches sprawling around the bottle and distant mountains at the back, on one side a monkey sitting at the crotch of the pine tree looking up at a bee, some lingzhi *funguses growing underneath, a zigzag stream flowing down the mountain, on the other side a dark brown horse standing under the pine branches and a dedicatory inscription dated and signed "made by Ye Zhongsan at Dumen (the capital) in the autumn of 1895, for assessment by the respected uncle Boliang," amber stopper with a tiny pearl finial and black vinyl collar.*

Light brown crystal, of flattened rounded rectangular shape on a ring foot, painted in bright colors with a garden scene continuing on both sides, on one side children playing with lanterns and attended by a woman, on the reverse children imitating a stage play and an inscription reading "made by Ye Zhongsan in the mid-spring of 1917," followed by a red seal with the character yin *(seal), light blue glass stopper with blue vinyl collar.*

AS MENTIONED PREVIOUSLY, YE ZHONGSAN was especially renowned for his narrative figure paintings. He liked to choose episodes from novels, folklore, and legends or even daily lives. His figures are largely in the style of the painter Ren Bonian (1840–96) of the Shanghai School, and they are applied with bright colors, achieving highly dramatic effects. Such an approach became characteristic of his style and later the inherent practice of his family workshop, the Apricot Grove Studio. Two elder sons carried on this tradition, and while faithful to their father's standard, they occasionally produced new compositions or even new subjects. But prior to 1949 almost all their bottles were signed with their father's name, Ye Zhongsan, making it difficult to distinguish the work of one from the other and consequently they are generally grouped as from the "Ye Studio." The eldest son, Ye Bengzhen, started painting around 1912, with the active period of the studio commonly accepted as extending from 1912 to 1949. The present bottle, an example from this period, bears the trademark signature Ye Zhongsan.

Although the sons scrupulously followed the father's style, some slight differences between their works and his can be discerned by close examination. Whereas the father provided more complex, realistic landscape settings, the sons tended to use a simpler open ground or, later, even flat settings. Whereas the father applied detailed brushstrokes to depict various textures of plants and rocks, the sons comparatively limited their brushworks to short straight strokes for grass or tree barks and short curvy strokes for leaves and rocks. Whereas the father outlined his figures in rather straight lines and tended to use many small right angles for the folds of clothes, after Ren Bonian's figure style, the sons drew longer and softer outlines, and they rendered the folds of clothes with rounder curves. The father liked to use bright orange-red colors but his overall palette was rather subdued, featuring gradational pale blue and slate; the sons used comparatively brighter and stronger colors in flat application. And finally, both inscription and signature appear to be written in slightly different manners.[1]

The clever position of the large tree in this example is worth noting. Its towering and bending pose helps to separate clearly the ground from the sky, not only solidifying the open ground where the children play, but also suggesting the infinite sky in the background. To our delight, this three-dimensional effect is further enhanced when the bottle is seen against light.

The painting of children cavorting with lanterns conveys the cheerful air of the Chinese *Yuanxiao* festival, which is celebrated on the fifteenth day of the first lunar month when the moon is full. As realistically recorded here, children would traditionally play with colorful lanterns of various designs, some taking the shape of auspicious motifs like fish, symbolizing abundance. A similarly lively atmosphere is created in the scene on the reverse, where children imitate a stage play. Some beat a drum and gong, some wave a banner and brandish a spear, while others applaud and watch attentively, their vivid gestures and expressions all caught as if a snapshot had been taken at that very moment.

Notes
1. For the father's figure paintings, see Hui and Sin, *An Imperial Qing Tradition,* no. 230–33; Lawrence, *Miniature Masterpieces,* no. 136; and Sin et al., eds., *A Congregation of Snuff Bottle Connoisseurs,* nos. 299–300. For those of the Ye Studio, see relevant figures in Hugh Moss, "The Apricot Grove Studio: The Works of the Ye Family, The Artists," *Journal of the International Chinese Snuff Bottle Society* 16, no. 1 (Spring 1984): 55–72.

THE SIMPLIFIED FORMS AND, ON ONE SIDE, interior setting seen on this bottle embody a new interest of the Ye Studio in flat compositions. The painting represents two areas, one inside a room and one seen through a window; however, pictorial space is not depicted by plastic forms but simply suggested with bold lines. Using only one diagonal line, the artist separated the left wall from the ground floor; similarly two lines meeting at a right angle indicate a window as well as distinguish the side from the back wall. The artist employed only two cool shades of pale gray and white for the entire setting. The pictorial space can be logically perceived, but it is essentially flat since the walls, window, and floor exist on the same plane. Against this flat and monochromatic ground, the artist set four figures, a table, and a drum-shaped stool in plastic forms and bright colors. Such a deliberate contrast in form and color, in conjunction with the deceptively simple composition, marks a new aesthetic sensibility and stylistic character of the Ye Studio.

On the reverse, the painting displays more depth. Two distinct spaces are clearly partitioned by the railing painted in red and bluish green. The pictorial distance beyond the railing is subtly suggested by the light green of leaves and grass.

44 | INSIDE-PAINTED SNUFF
BOTTLE
First month of spring, 1923
From the Ye Studio
H. 2⅜ in. (6.7 cm)
96.39.32

Rock crystal, of flattened rounded rectangular shape on a ring foot, painted in colors with two episodes from the novel Dream of the Red Chamber *(Honglou Meng) of the late eighteenth century, on one side with four figures in an interior setting, titled* Lin Xiaoxiang kuiduo juhua shi *(Lin Xiaoxiang won the poem competition on the theme of chrysanthemum) and signed "made by Ye Zhongsan in the first month of the spring of 1923," followed with a red seal with the character* yin *(seal), the reverse side with three figures in a garden, titled* Baochai jieshan jidai shuangqiao *(Baochai ridiculed both Baoyu and Daiyu on the pretext of finding a fan), dark green glass stopper.*

THE LANDSCAPE PAINTING OF THIS BOTTLE IS DISTINCTLY after the style of Zhou Leyuan.[1] The broad river lying tranquilly in the middle separates the gentle sloping mountains in the distance from the grassy mounds at the foreground. The scene is presented in the familiar "three-distance" composition, yet individual elements are well formed and smoothly integrated. The fine brushwork is skillfully and confidently executed to successfully bring forth various forms and textures. Light tones of ink black and bluish green imbue the scene with an air of spring. In such genial natural surroundings, where the grass has just turned green and the spring breeze just begun to blow, nothing could make a man happier than to play a favorite musical instrument or to take a leisurely, carefree walk, as the scholar depicted in the painting. It represents a typical, elegant literati taste.

From about 1912 to 1929 the Ye Studio made bottles in the style of Zhou Leyuan in almost every time-honored subject. Many are of high quality and all are signed with the father's name, Ye Zhongsan. It is often impossible to identify the individual artist of a particular bottle, but careful comparison of the brushwork and calligraphy of this bottle with the later works of the second son, Ye Xiaofeng (1900–1971), suggests that he probably painted this bottle.

Notes
1. A dated (1891) bottle by Zhou, decorated on one side with the same scene of a pavilion in landscape, is in the collection of the Palace Museum, Beijing. See Xia, ed., *Masterpieces of Snuff Bottles in the Palace Museum*, no. 209.

45 | INSIDE-PAINTED SNUFF
BOTTLE
Fifth month, 1927
From the Ye Studio
H. 3 in. (7.6 cm)
96.39.30

Light brown crystal, of upright rectangular shape on a ring foot, painted in elegant colors with a riverscape continuing on both sides, on one side a man holding a staff walking along the waterfront followed by a boy holding a zither, the reverse with an empty pavilion on a mound by tall pine trees, signed "made by Ye Zhongsan in the fifth month of 1927 in Beijing," and a red seal with the character yin *(seal), coral-colored glass stopper with silver collar.*

46 | INSIDE-PAINTED SNUFF
BOTTLE
c. 1970s–80s
By Liu Shouben
H. 2⁵⁄₁₆ in. (5.9 cm)
96.39.39

Rock crystal, of circular shape with a small indented oval base, painted in colors on both sides, on one side a pond scene with two water buffaloes each carrying a boy and some reeds at the far distance, on the reverse a white horse standing by the waterfront and an aged willow tree with tender leaves, signed "made by Liu Shouben in Beijing" and a red seal with the character yin *(seal), red agate stopper.*

LIU SHOUBEN (B. 1943) BECAME A PUPIL of Ye Xiaofeng in 1960 at the age of seventeen. After learning and mastering the Ye tradition, he began to show his versatility and gradually formed his own distinctive style.

In early works such as the present one, traces of the Ye family influence can be clearly observed. Both the motifs and the color application are unmistakably that of the Ye tradition. Yet with its slightly sparser composition and lighter tones, the painting imparts a fresher and airy atmosphere.

Of snow white with emerald green inclusions, carved in the round in the form of two badgers, on the back of one a bat carved in relief and on the tail of the other a lingzhi *fungus carved in relief.*

47 | CARVED JADEITE TOGGLE
18th–19th century
H. 2 in. (5.7 cm)
96.39.51

IT IS PURELY DUE TO ITS LOVELINESS AND MINIATURE quality that this charming jadeite carving was included in the Thal gift of snuff bottles to the museum. The motif of two badgers prevailed in Chinese decorative arts of the Qing dynasty and was frequently seen in jade or quartz toggles as well as inside-painted bottles. Here, the two badgers are carved with consummate skill. Their bodies are realistically sculpted in rounded forms with raised and indented planes to suggest strong muscles. Facial and body features are detailed with incised lines, and the stone is excellently polished to bring an unctuous sheen to the surface.

The design demonstrates an ingenious use of natural material. The green and pure white colors originally converged in the middle of the stone. By choosing this point to carve the legs of the badgers in openwork, the artist succeeded in visually separating the animals while necessarily connecting them. The idea of being a whole is indispensable to the subject. Badgers are said to often curl up so that the muzzle of one rests on the hindquarters of the other. The image of two badgers thus symbolizes marital felicities. As the Chinese word for "badger" *(huan)* is phonetically identical with another word meaning "to be happy" *(huan),* two badgers thus form a pun as "double happinesses" *(shuanghuan).* This delightful meaning makes the present carving a fitting object to conclude this catalogue. For the artist, it must have been a double happiness to produce not only a practical item but an artwork. For the family of the collector, it may also have been a double happiness to assemble a remarkable collection of precious artworks of a single category, and in doing so to embrace a wide spectrum of the artistic media of late imperial China.

Selected Bibliography

Fuller, Richard. *Chinese Snuff Bottles in the Seattle Art Museum*. Seattle: Seattle Art Museum, 1970.

Hui, Humphrey and Christopher Sin. *An Imperial Qing Tradition*. Hong Kong: Humphrey Hui and Christopher Sin, 1994.

Journal of the International Snuff Bottle Society. Baltimore, 1969–.

Kleiner, Robert. *Chinese Snuff Bottles*. Hong Kong: Oxford University Press, 1994.

Lawrence, Clare. *Miniature Masterpieces*. London: Zhenliu Xuan Publishing, 1996.

Little, Stephen, and Joseph Silver. *The World in a Bottle*. Hong Kong: Joseph Baruch Silver, 1994.

Moss, Hugh. "The Apricot Grove Studio." Parts 1–5. *Journal of the International Chinese Snuff Bottle Society* 14, no. 1 (Spring 1982): 1–8; no. 3 (Autumn 1982): 9–47; 16, no. 1 (Spring 1984): 49–72; 17, no. 1 (Spring 1985): 99–117; 17, no. 3 (Autumn 1985): 116–30.

Moss, Hugh, Victor Graham, and Ka Bo Tsang. *A Treasury of Chinese Snuff Bottles: The Mary and George Bloch Collection*. Vol. Jade. Hong Kong: Herald International, 1995.

Perry, Lilla. *Chinese Snuff Bottles: The Adventure and Studies of A Collector*. Rutland: Charles Tuttle, 1960.

Sin, Christopher, Humprey Hui, and Po Ming Kwong, eds. *A Congregation of Snuff Bottle Connoisseurs*. Hong Kong: C. A. Design, 1996.

Stevens, Bob C. *The Collector's Book of Snuff Bottles*. New York: Weatherhill, 1980.

Xia Gengqi, ed. *Masterpieces of Snuff Bottles in the Palace Museum* (Gugong Biyanhu Xuancui). Beijing: Forbidden City Publishing, 1995.

Zhang Linsheng. "A Study on the Manufacture of Snuff Bottles of the Qing Court" (Qinggong Biyanhu Zhiqi Kao). *The National Palace Museum Research Quarterly* (Gugong Xueshu Jikan) (Taipei) 8, no. 2, (1990): 1–39.

———, ed. *Snuff Bottles in the Collection of the National Palace Museum* (Gugong Biyanhu). Taipei: National Palace Museum, 1991.